# DISCOVERY OF LURAY CAVERNS, VIRGINIA

Russell H. Gurnee

Other books by Russell H. Gurnee:

*Cave Life* (with Charles E. Mohr)
*Visiting American Caves* (with Howard N. Sloane)
*Discovery at the Rio Camuy* (with Jeanne Gurnee)

# DISCOVERY OF LURAY CAVERNS, VIRGINIA

Russell H. Gurnee

R. H. GURNEE, INC. · CLOSTER, NEW JERSEY

*Library of Congress Cataloging in Publication Data*

Gurnee, Russell H.
    Discovery of Luray caverns, Virginia.

    Includes index.
    1. Luray Caverns, Va.   I. Title.
GB606.L87G87     917.55'94     78-3536
ISBN 0-931402-01-8     ISBN 0-931402-00-x pbk.

Printed in the United States of America

# INTRODUCTION

In 1878, the Shenandoah Valley of Virginia was slowly recuperating from the wounds of the War between the States. The scars on the landscape were healing, but the scars left by the human tragedy that had pitted brother against brother were still grievous. Economically the valley had been laid bare. The fields recovered, but the isolation from the mainstream of business left the smaller towns off the main roads struggling to survive. The State of Virginia had been readmitted to the Union in 1870. The railroad men of the North saw this as an opportunity to tap the raw materials of the South and exploit the labor market that had been left unemployed after the War.

Capitalists from Philadelphia and Baltimore convinced the readmitted State and the voters of Page County that if they would float a bond the company would build a railroad through the Shenandoah Valley, routing it along the east side of the Massanutten Ridge through the county seat of Luray. This would parallel the old route of the Baltimore and Ohio Railroad which traversed the west side of the Ridge. Two hundred thousand dollars were pledged by the voters and the railroad started. Unfortunately, the bonds were never issued and the company ran out of money. For seven years the roadbeds and road cuts sprouted weeds and brush. The citizens of Page County hoped that the time was imminent when the work would be renewed. The completion of the tracks and the coming of the steam engines became a goal that they believed would change the fortunes of all. But still the railroad did not come.

Farmers and businessmen clung to their resources as long as they could in the hopes of better times. When they could wait no longer, they moved west. This migration was not restricted to the Shenandoah Valley, for the war provided hard times in the North as well. Poverty at home always seemed harder than poverty someplace else, so families packed up their belongings and moved someplace else on the assumption that "it had to be better."

Benton Pixley Stebbins was one such migrant. Born in New York State in 1825, he worked on his family's farm until he was twenty-one. A restless man, he began to travel to seek his fortune. He worked as a carpenter, taught school, published a newspaper, and finally became a photographer. He married, and reared seven children, and then, at the age of fifty, he divorced his wife. With his photographic studio, he set out through the towns of New York. After marrying a distant cousin, Amelia Stebbins, he went to Easton, Maryland, still searching for that elusive fortune. In Easton he found only grief and disappointment when Amelia's parents, who had accompanied them to Maryland, both contracted malaria and died. They moved on, this time West: Benton, Amelia, their two-year-old son Eugene, and Amelia's sister and brother-in-law, Emily and Charles Vorhees.

They set out for the Shenandoah Valley after reading the railroad brochures stating that this was a favorable and fertile land. The brochures did not mention that this was a desperately poor region, so they set out with the same high hopes and wistful confidence that the residents of the Shenandoah Valley had as they left for their "land of promise" even farther west.

The two families made the journey over the Blue Ridge mountains in wagons with all of their possessions. After a five-day trip they reached the little town of Luray, Virginia. It was dark when they arrived; the journey had been long and difficult. The two families decided to stay in Luray, the county seat of Page County, and see if this might be where they could "find their fortune."

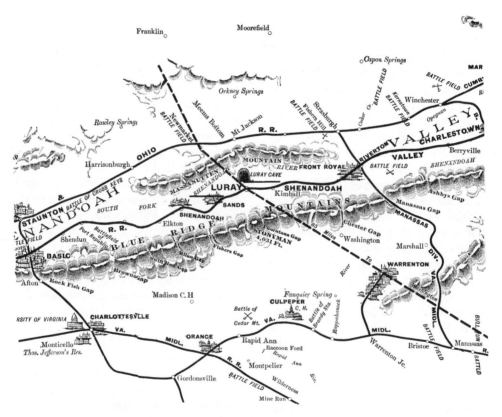

*The Shenandoah Valley Railroad, as completed in 1881, opened the Page Valley to direct traffic. At the time of Benton Stebbins' journey to the area the roadbed had been cleared to the town of Shenandoah, Virginia.*

# I

Benton Stebbins opened the hotel door to the street. On this July morning in 1878, all was quiet. The wind had died down during the night, and the soft glow from the east reflected a pink light off the Blue Ridge Mountains and the clouds. Buildings on both sides of the main street stood out in sharp silhouette. He breathed in deeply the early summer air and looked with an experienced eye at the buildings and houses. His occupation as a traveling photographer had taken him to hundreds of towns in the past five years and he liked to analyze the prosperity of an area when he arrived. This was important if he was to seize any opportunity that might be available to sell his product and replenish his dwindling pocketbook.

His wife Amelia and son Eugene were still sleeping in the hotel, for he wanted to look around before the activities of the day prevented an unhurried evalutation.

There were no continuous boardwalks, so Stebbins walked down the center of the street. While his gait was that of a young man, his hand hung loosely at his side—the result of an old injury. There were various business signs on either side: Dry Goods, General Merchandise, Hardware, two lawyers and one doctor. He did not see a sign for a photographer.

He paused at Hawksbill Creek, a tributary of the South Fork of the Shenandoah River. There was a good flow of water bank to bank and from the bridge he could clearly see the bottom. The water was only a few feet deep with cobbles and stones sharply visible in the early morning light. The bridge had recently been rebuilt and the acrid odor of tar and freshly sawed oak hung in the air. The oak structure had not yet weathered to the mottled gray of most country bridges.

Across the bridge was a hill. The sun burst forth over the Blue Ridge, lighting up the buildings and reflecting off the white gravestones in the cemetery on the right. The road had been leveled at this point, but he could see by the piles of pine ties that this was designed to be the roadbed of a railroad. A sign on a small red shed said "Shenandoah Valley Railroad," confirming his opinion. Apparently there had been a halt in activity, for weeds had grown up around the building and the ties had begun to weather.

Stebbins knew that the completion of the railroad would change the entire economic picture of this sleeping town.

*Benton Pixley Stebbins, co-discoverer of Luray Caverns, Virginia*

He had seen that happen in Pennsylvania when the railroad, extended to the oil fields near Titusville, had turned the rural farming area into a boom town almost overnight. Fortunes were made as property values soared, and for enterprising businessmen there were opportunities (and risks) available. This, the discovery of the railbed, was the most exciting part of his early morning walk. Here was an opportunity and potential that he had overlooked the night before when they came into town.

*Amelia Stebbins, wife of Benton Stebbins, artist and illustrator*

After a hearty breakfast with Amelia and Eugene, he obtained a newspaper, the *Page-Courier*. A four page-weekly published every Thursday, it covered national and state news on page one, the country and political news on page two and had local news and advertising on pages three and four. Stebbins was pleased to learn there was no photographer in town; there was an advertisement for a studio in Front Royal, twenty miles to the north. He was also excited to read that the Shenandoah Railroad,

after two years delay, was to begin laying track again, and it was estimated the line would reach Luray by September. The roadbed he had seen was completed to the town of Shenandoah, about twenty miles south, to the Shenandoah Iron Mines. This rich deposit required a railroad if it were to prove successful. At present, pig iron produced in the furnaces was transported by wagon over Massanutten Mountain to New Market where it was loaded and shipped to mills.

Reinforced with this information and buoyed with the optimism of his naturally ebullient spirit, Stebbins gathered together a portfolio of photographs and sought the office of the *Page-Courier*.

"My name is Stebbins," he said to a slender, sandy haired young man with a white shirt. "Are you the editor?"

"No, Andrew Broaddus is the editor," the young man replied, wiping his hands on his apron. "I'm T. J. Berrey, assistant editor; Mr. Broaddus is not in. Can I help you?"

Stebbins placed his portfolio on the counter and looked over the shoulder of the young man to the back of the shop where a boy was cleaning the printing press. It looked like a fine working shop. Stebbins had been part owner of the *Corry City News* in Pennsylvania; the scene was a familiar one to him.

"I'd like to place an ad in your paper," Stebbins said. "We just arrived in town last night and it will take a few days to set up the studio. I'm a photographer and my wife is an artist. We are thinking of settling here in Luray for a while."

As he spoke, he spread some photographs on the counter. There were small portraits of children in christening dresses, wedding photos, pictures of a group of men standing stiffly in front of a frame building, and scenes of farm buildings with the family on the front porch. Mr Berrey bent over to study the sepia-colored photographs and nodded approvingly as he went from one to the other. Stebbins then placed several large portraits on the counter. These had been tinted in a wash polychrome, giving flesh tone and life to the features and color to the subjects' clothing.

"We specialize in photo-chrome oil pictures, and in gem and ferrotypes," he said.

Mr. Berrey picked several of the photographs and took them to the window for closer examination.

"They're excellent! I've never seen better, even in cities," said Mr. Berrey enthusiastically. "Where is your studio?"

"We're staying at Washington House. But I would like to move to a rooming house where it would be less expensive to live while we set up our studio," replied Stebbins, pleased with the assistant editor's response to his work.

"You might be able to stay with the widow Duncan. She has some rooms available, on East Main Street, just the other side of the church," supplied Mr. Berrey.

Stebbins noted this, and then discussed further some of the pictures and the techniques in using the Stereo camera. After a few minutes Stebbins asked for some paper and wrote out an advertisement to be placed in the Page Courier starting with the next issue, June 27, 1878.

## OF INTEREST TO ALL

It is with pleasure that we inform the citizens of Luray and vicinity, that we have our portable Photograph and Art Gallery completed and we are now ready to take all kinds of Pictures known in the Art Gems, Ferrotypes, Photographs and &c. &c.

Copying and enlarging done to order. All our work guaranteed or no pay asked. We make a speciality of Crystal, or Photo Chrome Oil Pictures, also landscapes and Portraits in oil colors.

Soliciting your patronage, we subscribe ourselves your obedient servant,

B. P. Stebbins.

Mr. Berrey read the ad, and counted up the words. "That will be two dollars for one insertion, one dollar for each additional insertion."

Stebbins thought of his dwindling finances. With some reluctance he counted out the four dollars for three weeks from his shrinking bankroll.

Meanwhile Amelia and Eugene had been out to see the town. When Stebbins returned they went to see the widow Duncan about a room and to find a location for their gallery. Emily and Charles Voorhees, Amelia's sister and brother-in-law, had also been busy. Charles found a temporary job helping Samuel Judd in his harness shop. It paid fifty cents a day; he considered himself lucky to have the position while he looked around for a farm.

Mrs. Duncan, a motherly lady, kept a neat house and flower garden. She was pleased to show them the second floor bedroom area, provide space in the barn for the horses, and permit them to set up a studio in the adjacent lot. Amelia looked pleased with the arrangements; so Stebbins agreed to the terms of $3.50 per week, for both room and board.

Amelia was tired of traveling with the portable studio. It had been romantic in the first summer of their marriage, but the inconvenience of accommodations and the uncertainties of the profession became a burden to her. She tried to do whatever Stebbins wanted, but she desired a more permanent home. She felt that Eugene needed playmates, and she hoped that the move to Luray might last more than the several weeks that Stebbins suggested. Stebbins also desired a steadier income and a more profitable life. For many years he had lived by his wits, continually exploring any possibilities of advancement.

Emptying out the wagon, settling into the house, and setting up the dark room tent required several days. Amelia cherished a small Mason and Hamlin pump organ that originally belonged to her mother. This instrument had been carefully stored in the wagon, but they needed that space to run the studio. Mrs. Duncan admired the organ so much she agreed to put it in the parlor on the first floor. After it was in place, Amelia tried it out. When the windy, reedy notes of "Rock of Ages" poured out, the widow was captivated and delighted that the organ would be in her parlor. Amelia knew that her ability on the reed organ, though limited to a few of the well-known hymns, had always proved to be a successful introduction to a new community. With the pump organ on the ground floor, the family on the second floor and the horses in the barn, Stebbins felt pleased that he had established his base of operations.

But his concern for business prospects caused him sleepless nights. He made the rounds of the churches, met all the ministers, and left his card in the hope that there might be a wedding or christening before the advertisement appeared in the paper. He visited each merchant on Main Street. His approach was a soft one, and his speech was slow and deliberate.

His ear for mimicry helped him to adopt the accent of the area and be less conspicuous when talking with local people. He had spent several years in

Louisana before the Civil War, and three years in Maryland. It was difficult to identify the region of his background, so he answered any questions of where he came from with "Easton, Maryland, Talbot County."

While he was setting up the tent on the lot next to the Duncan place, he was visited by a young, dark-haired man who approached him with some diffidence.

"Mr. Stebbins?" he inquired, then with more confidence, "I wonder if you'd like to look at some of my pictures?"

"Why certainly; let's get out of the sun," replied Stebbins as he motioned him toward the porch.

"I'm Billy Campbell; my father is the sheriff. I've been interested in photography for a couple of years, but there

*William B. Campbell, co-discoverer of Luray Caverns and son of Sheriff Campbell*

ain't nobody around here that has done much with it." He opened an envelope and brought out several photographs.

Stebbins held the pictures carefully by the edges. One at a time with his good left hand he held them out at arm's

*Burnt district of the Main Street of Luray. Photo by Bushong and Campbell, 1877.*

length to inspect each, then placed them in a row on the porch. He put on his glasses and examined them more carefully.

The pictures were all of the town of Luray, four of them of a devastated area, still smoking, that Stebbins did not recognize. He looked inquiringly at Billy.

"That's the burnt district on the south side of Main Street. Last winter it burned out," Bill said. "Doc Brumback and Doc Miller lost all of their equipment, Jim Modisett his furniture, Lawyer Welfley his papers, and oh yes, Mr. Litchliter lost his whole saddle shop. It was a terrible fire. Some of it has been rebuilt, but the Union Hotel was completely gone and it don't look as if it will be rebuilt."

"Jim Bushong and I took the pictures," added Billy. "We had them for sale, but we didn't sell many."

Stebbins murmured his regrets, said that they were fine pictures, and asked how could he help him.

"Well, I'd like to learn more about photography. Jim moved to Front Royal and since it was his camera and equipment I haven't had a chance to do any more work."

"What are you doing now, Billy?" asked Stebbins.

"Working on the farm, but I'd like to learn more about taking pictures."

"It's not an easy profession. Photography is easy to learn, but selling and getting the people to want the pictures is not, as times are not good and people don't have money to spend for what some call 'foolishness.' I wouldn't recommend it for a profession in these hard times." As he said that Stebbins saw the disappointment in Billy's eyes and realized that he had made a mistake.

He thought of his limited means, and that this might be an opportunity to gain a pupil, so he hastened to add, "But you have real talent here with these pictures. We would be happy to have you take some lessons and we could teach you some of the newest methods. What kind of equipment did Bushong have?''

Billy willingly launched into a description, and the two men discussed the techniques of the photographic art. Stebbins assumed the role of teacher and Billy happily fell into the role of student.

The days passed quickly. Stebbins, with the assistance of his first pupil, obtained several commissions at the tannery for Peter B. Borst, and also a few portraits of the daughters of some of the town's more affluent citizens. But there was no great enthusiasm for the new business.

The gossip at the general store of W. C. Alther still centered around the rail-

to Front Royal and beyond. It was from there that the tracks would have to be laid first. The *Great Eastern* came once a day from Sperryville to the east, the most direct route for news from Washington, D.C., and it brought its supply of gossip for the town.

The citizens of Page County had made a firm commitment to the railroad seven years before by public referendum to underwrite $200,000 worth of bonds of the Shenandoah Valley Railroad. The railroad pledged to build the line down Page Valley east of Massanutten Ridge and through Luray rather than down the main valley to the west. The commitment had not been fulfilled, either by the railroad or by the issuance of bonds; and

*W. C. Alther's General Merchandise Store, Main Street, Luray, Virginia*

road. Stage coach drivers and passengers brought the latest news. West from New Market, Gil Zirkle's coach Fast Line made the three-hour trip twice a day, bringing news. The *Lightning Express* and the *Comfortable Passenger Accommodation Hack* came from Front Royal to the north. This was the best source of news, as the road bed, now covered with weeds, was completed

the people of Page County were having doubts about the wisdom of a tax burden that might have no benefits. The impasse slowed the work of the Shenandoah Railroad which was without sufficient money—and the expenses of bridges, track, and other specialized labor lay ahead.

Speculation of the good times to come with the railroad obsessed the town.

Strangers to the town were objects of curiosity because of the limited access, and the smartly dressed visitor was thought to be "from the railroad." If he was sufficiently well dressed, he might even be classed as a "capitalist." In a town of fewer than six hundred, any visitor was immediately recognized and the ability to gauge his position (and relation to the railroad) became a local sport.

Stebbins, with his peaceable manner and dignified appearance, was soon accepted by the local gentry as an asset to the community. In discussions at Alther's Store in the evenings, he spoke of the surrounding countryside, and his interests in the local geography and geology.

He limited his political discussions to a few statements against the "sins of liquor" since the town of Luray had been dry for the past four years, and temperance was accepted by most. This stance helped him with the town council and the influential men of the church.

Stebbins felt if the railroad were to come there would be an opportunity for natural attractions to win the attention of visitors and make a lot of money for the promoters. One of the selling points for the railroad to consider the eastern route had been access to Weyer's Cave, forty miles south of Luray in Augusta County. Discovered in 1802, this cave was a destination for many travelers. The cave's attraction provided much needed income for the local area during the hard times following the Civil War. The discovery of Fountain Cave, only a short distance from Weyer's Cave, caused renewed interest, and speculations about the rail line.

Stebbins queried the crowd gathered at Alther's Store if they knew of any cave in the limestone hills around Luray. As a stranger in town only ten days he felt he could learn more at these informal sessions than from personal exploration.

Trent Lillard and Billy Campbell spent their free days hunting and poking around the woods outside of town and told Stebbins of an "old cave" about a mile away atop Cave Hill. Most of the men present had been partway into the cave, a local landmark, or said they had. With an interested audience they became eloquent about its beauties—real, or embellished by retelling.

"The cave was discovered more than seventy years ago by a hunter. It was on the Ruffner place so it has been called Ruffner's Cave ever since," offered one of the men.

"It's a grand cave," said Billy. "I've been in it with my Uncle Andrew. It's got wondrous rooms and it goes under the whole hill, nobody knows how far." The normally shy and quiet Billy warmed up to his subject and became excited as he recalled trips made a few years ago.

"You need a rope to get to the entrance, then down a steep slope to a muddy and rock floor. It's dark and gloomy in the entrance, but the next room is something huge. It's called the Congress and covers nearly an acre. There are huge columns and pillars that you go through into the Glazed Room and Masonic Hall."

Billy paused, other men nodded, and Isaac Williams added, "I knew Will Harris who said he had explored there in 1825. It was something fine then, but there have been lots of pillars broke since then. He told me that there was wonderful sights—like the stone that looked like a human heart, all red and dripping."

"It ain't been completely explored neither," ventured Trent Lilliard. "My father said that he went in there and if he didn't have a string he never would have found his way out.''

Stebbins' unusual interest in the stories led Billy and Trent to agree to take him to the cave the next day. When Stebbins went home he told Amelia of his intended adventure. She cautioned him to be careful, but said nothing further.

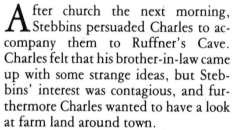

# II

After church the next morning, Stebbins persuaded Charles to accompany them to Ruffner's Cave. Charles felt that his brother-in-law came up with some strange ideas, but Stebbins' interest was contagious, and furthermore Charles wanted to have a look at farm land around town.

The four men, dressed in rough clothes, took the New Market road toward Cave Hill. They carried candles and matches, an ax, and a coil of heavy rope. In the country the corn was knee-high along the road, and several untilled fields were fenced so cattle could graze and forage. At the highest point of the road they could see Massanutten Ridge, green and slightly misty in the bright sunlight. Billy turned up a wagon road, skirting a huge depression with a little pond at the bottom.

"That's the biggest sinkhole in the county," said Billy. "It don't ever seem to get any more than a few feet of water in it. We don't know where it goes or why it don't flood in the spring."

The depression, eighty feet deep and nearly a thousand feet across, was smooth-sided without ledges or outcrops of rock—a natural basin without any visible outlet. The men followed the wagon road toward the top of the hill, into a stand of tall pine trees perched on the summit like a Mohegan Indian haircut. The trees had grown to full height. It was evident that this land had not been pastured as the rocky trail passed sinkholes and ledges.

Billy led them off the trail to a sinkhole with steep exposed sides. He waited for the others to gather around him. The crevice-like hole descended into the blackness of Ruffner's Cave. Billy picked up a stone and tossed it into the pit. It ricocheted against the side as it bounded down a slope in the distance. There were no foot- or hand-holds in the pit for about twenty feet, and the bottom sloped off to the far side of the opening like an open well. Charles laid down the rope and looked at the pit with little enthusiasm.

"We ain't going down there, are we?" he asked.

Billy and Trent didn't answer for they were looking at a pine tree about six inches in diameter to aid in their descent. Trent took the ax, and went to work. With his many years' experience clearing land and cutting firewood the tree was soon toppled. He trimmed the branches and then, with a practiced eye, began to chop notches every twelve inches up the trunk. He cut about twenty steps in the tree, and then with two sharp blows cut off the slender end. Trent was sweating when he finished, but not winded.

They all dragged the tree to the edge of the pit and lowered it into place. Adjusting it to the right angle and driving it into the leaves and debris at the bottom took almost as long as it had taken Trent to cut it. Billy tested the pole with his weight, then jumped up and down on the top step.

"It's safe," he assured his companions.

Stebbins tied the rope to a tree and threw the coil into the black pit. The rope hit and slithered out of sight. It snapped taut and then sagged slightly as it arched down the hole.

"Billy, why don't you and Trent go down first; Charles and I will follow," said Stebbins.

Billy took candles and matches out of the sack and divided them among the men, three apiece. He stuffed the extra candles in his pocket to leave his hands free, grasped the rope as a safety line, and stepped off backward onto the makeshift ladder. He eased onto the first steps carefully, but soon realized it was safe and quickly descended to the slope below. Pausing to light a candle, and holding the rope, he disappeared into the darkness. Only the twitching of the rope showed his progress to the men at the top. The rope went slack and a call from below told them to come along.

Trent followed the same path as Billy, paused to light his candle, and disappeared.

The descent would be more difficult for Stebbins. He watched the others carefully until they were out of sight. The injury that had twisted his right hand did not leave him enough strength even to grasp a pencil, although he had learned to write with his left hand. He had to grasp the rope to aid his descent.

Holding the rope in his left hand, he put the candle between his teeth, and gingerly proceeded down the slender pole. At the foot of the sapling he gripped the rope and slid down the slope.

Charles joined them, and as their eyes became adjusted to the darkness, the light of the four candles revealed a passage continuing downward. Billy went ahead. His light reflected off the ceiling and convoluted walls giving the waiting men the impression they were looking down a narrow river gorge. The walls were wet and glistening; the floor slippery and mud-covered. The rope did not reach the bottom, but it was easy to scramble the last few feet down to where the floor leveled.

"Halooo!" shouted Billy, startling his companions as the echoes rolled back from the blackness. The true size of the room was lost in the void. There was no form, shape, or definition to the room, but only darkness as the candles were unable to penetrate the gloom.

Charles was uncomfortable. He was not frightened, but did not like the feeling of being enclosed in this chambered rock. He said nothing, but sat quietly near the entrance to the room. Trent and Billy were having a fine time as they moved to remote parts of the room, holding up their candles to cast light on the walls. The floor was a jumbled mass of broken rock. The center had a high mound of breakdown which centuries before had fallen from the domed ceiling above. Billy left one candle at the far side of the room, and another at the top of the center mound. The room appeared to be about fifty feet wide and eighty feet long, and rose forty feet to the ceiling above the mountain where Billy stood.

Stebbins had never been in a cave this large before. In New York State he had crawled into a few crevices and chased rabbits down limestone sinkholes, but he had never seen anything this big. It was spectacular.

"Halooo!" he cried, startling Charles as the echoes rolled back. Excitement gripped him as he cast off his dignified air and felt like a boy again. With his candle he peered into shadows on the walls, examining the glistening crystals that covered portions of the breakdown. Muddy footprints on the white patches of flowstone, many broken formations, and names written in bold smoky letters on the nearly white walls gave evidence that many people had visited the cave. Careful examination showed that there were two descending passages leading from the room, and one balcony that had a few stalactites and stalagmites. It was as Billy said: "A grand and gloomy cave."

Charles was becoming restless, and his inactivity was causing him to become chilled. He was glad when the three others turned back to the entrance. The rope and notched pole made an easy exit, but all were surprised and stunned by the sweltering 90 degrees that greeted them on the surface. The sun was low in the west, but the heat of the day continued to be oppressive as the tired group returned to Luray that Sunday evening in July of 1878.

Benton Stebbins had been captivated by the cave. His interest in nature and his sense of a possible economic opportunity added to the experience. He was not knowledgeable of caves. He knew of the famed Mammoth Cave in Kentucky, and he had heard of Howe's Cave in New York, and now Weyer's Cave in Virginia. Ruffner's Cave was the largest cave he had ever seen. If he was excited about it, perhaps other people would be too—maybe enough to pay to see it. He knew that Weyer's Cave charged visitors seventy-five cents. Sometimes more than a hundred people came to see it on a weekend. In a few months the railroad would reach Luray. This could mean a continuous flow of tourists eager to see a natural wonder only a mile from the station.

Stebbins did not sleep well. The unaccustomed exertion and the excitement of a possible business venture kept his mind active. He woke Amelia and told her his plan. She listened patiently, then dismissed it with a tired shrug. Alone he continued to reflect on his visions of wealth and success.

The next day Stebbins suggested to Billy that they search for another entrance to Ruffner's Cave so the public could see it without the exertions of the rope and ladder. The plan came as a surprise to Billy. He never thought people would pay good money to do what they did yesterday. When he realized that Stebbins was serious he suggested they visit his uncle Andrew J. Campbell. "He knows more about caves than anybody in the county," Billy declared.

Stebbins had met Andrew Campbell earlier. He rented the former tailor shop on Main Street and renamed it the New Era. There he did tinsmithing, downspouting, repaired roofs, and sold wood stoves. He learned this trade from Charles Keyser after he returned from service with the Page Grays and the 33rd Regiment. Andrew had two brothers, Thomas Rickey Campbell Sr., a storekeeper with the U. S. Government, and William Campbell Jr., Sheriff of Page County. Andrew, forty-two, was well known and liked in town.

At the New Era Billy and Stebbins found Andrew Campbell soldering up some drain pipe. The pungent odor of acid and sal ammoniac permeated the shop as he swabbed the metal with acid and skillfully ran a bead of solder around the joint. When Campbell finished he rinsed his hands in a bucket of water to remove the acid. Billy introduced Stebbins and recounted their trip to Ruffner's Cave.

"I think that with the railroad coming to Luray in a few months, a natural attraction like Ruffner's Cave would be a real moneymaker," said Stebbins directly.

"Well, it ain't much of a cave," observed Andrew. "It might have been once, but it is so badly used now nobody would give a tap to visit it."

ANDREW J. CAMPBELL.

*Andrew J. Campbell, co-discoverer of Luray Caverns and first man to enter the cave*

This statement was a disappointment and surprise to Stebbins. He had been impressed, and now to hear that the cave was not much was disturbing. "We hoped that you would be interested in exploring the old cave to look for another entrance and maybe finding more cave rooms," he said, not willing to give up.

"Well, it's possible that there is a big cave someplace near Luray," mused Andrew. "I might be interested in looking for a new one, but I'd not want to spend any time in the Old Cave. But a new cave with undamaged formations like Fountain Cave. . . . Now that would be something!" Andrew's face brightened with the prospect.

"We'll need some help," he continued. "We'd have to dig in some of the sinkholes if we hope to find anything new."

"We can get help from Trent Lilliard, Billy and yourself. That would split it four ways—enough for the work, but not too many for the profits," offered Stebbins.

"How about Charles Vorhees?" asked Billy. "Is he in it ?"

"No, I'm afraid that Charles doesn't care for caves much. He told me on the way home last night that he had been in two caves—his first and his last—all in the same day," said Stebbins.

It was difficult for all of them to get together. Business for Stebbins and Andrew was slow, but farm work for Billy and Trent was plentiful as the harvest season approached. Crops needed tending and of course the chores wouldn't quit. But finally a date was set for beginning the search.

For three July weekends they gathered the tools necessary to dig in sinkholes and other likely-looking places. Andrew had a list of prospective areas. At first they worked on Cave Hill, but with no luck. Andrew knew of several sinkholes near the Shenendoah River, so they spent two days in fruitless searches along the cliffs, and in the pastures near the banks. It was hot and discouraging work. At first local boys wanted to tag along, but when they were asked to dig and help drag out rocks thrown in the sinks by the farmers who cleared the land, the boys quit and went fishing in the Shenandoah River.

Everyone in town knew of the search. The evening's discussion at Alther's Store turned to likely places to look for caves.

After two weeks of little luck, the quartet began to be the butt of some good-natured ribbing.

"Have you thought of tying a string to the leg of a bat and following it home?" chided one of the regular loungers at Alther's.

"How about using a witch-hazel twig as a divining rod? Had a feller find water for my well that way. You might try it."

Three of the four searchers took it in good humor. They shrugged off being called "Cave Rats" when they walked back through town after a particularly strenuous day of digging.

Soon they became known as the "Phantom Chasers." Stebbins did not really mind the joking. It was innocent fun, provided visibility for him, and established an identity that he could not procure with newspaper advertising.

Trent did not like the joking. He was young, sensitive, and beginning to feel that this was all a futile effort. After a month he took Stebbins aside and said that he didn't want to look for the "big cave" any more. He wanted to tell Stebbins first, for he, as well as the others, had accepted Benton Stebbins as the leader of the party; it seemed natural that he discuss it with him before he brought it up with the others.

Stebbins could see that his group was falling apart, but without more assurance of success he couldn't blame Trent. The others understood, but decided they would try a few more days.

On the first of August, 1878, some encouraging news appeared. "Have you seen the paper?" Billy asked breathlessly as he ran up the walk to the Duncan house. Benton and Amelia were sitting on the porch in the early evening.

"Here, on page three," he said, pointing to an article in the lead column. Stebbins put on his glasses and read the article aloud to Amelia.

## A WONDERFUL CAVE
## A DISCOVERY MADE BY A POOR FARMER NEAR GLASGOW, KY.
### (from the Jefferson City Tribune.)

Another wonderful cave, says a correspondent of the Evening Post, has been discovered near Glasgow, Ky. It has already been explored for a distance of 25 miles in one direction called the "Long Route". The Avenues are very wide, and a span of horses can easily be drawn through for a distance of eleven miles. Three rivers, wide and very deep, are encountered in the "Long Route". One of them is navigable for fourteen miles until the passages become too narrow to admit a boat. The cave is wonderful beyond description and far supersedes in grandeur the Mammoth, or any cave before discovered.

"Isn't that just great!" interrupted Billy. "Go ahead, read on, it's better."

## SEVERAL MUMMIFIED REMAINS

Have been discovered in one of the large rooms. They were reposing in stone coffins, rudely constructed and from their appearance may have been in this cave for centuries. They present every appearance of Egyptian mummies. Great excitement prevails over this very important discovery. Mr. Edwin Mortimer of Chestnut Street, Louisville, Ky. purchased three of the mummies and has them now in his possession. Major George M. Proctor of Glasgow Junction, Ky. purchased the remainder of the mummies from the owner of the cave, whose name is Thomas Kelly. He is, or rather was, a few days ago, a very poor man, struggling to make a payment on a farm of twenty four acres upon which, by mere accident the entrance to this wonderful cave was discovered. He realized about $400 from the sale of the mummies, and is now offered $10,000 cash for the cave. The entrance to the cave is within the town limits and only about two miles walk from the depot. The newly discovered cave has been named the "GRAND CRYSTAL CAVE" and is as beautiful as the name implies. Ladders and bridges are being constructed, and as Mr. J. R. Puckett, a capitalist of the town, announces his intention of having a small steamboat constructed expressly for the purpose of navigating its wonderful rivers.

There was silence when Stebbins finished. All three were swept up with the vision of this wonderful discovery by a poor farmer, and the thought of $10,000 cash was breathtaking.

"Do you think we might find anything as grand as that?" asked Billy quietly.

"Well, it doesn't have to be that grand," said Stebbins. "It has to be a fine cave, but it doesn't have to be as grand as that." His voice trailed off.

The article affected Andrew as much as it had Billy and Stebbins. After a night's sleep and further study it appeared to Stebbins that the account might be a little exaggerated. He knew of journalistic license and thought that the cave could not be twenty-five miles long and still lie under twenty-four acres of land. But this doubt he kept to himself. His two partners were again fired up for the search. Besides, everyone in town had read the article and would not be so quick to make fun of their efforts.

In the past month Benton Stebbins had walked over most fields within a few miles of town. He had looked at the spring by Hawksbill Creek where reputedly corn cobs dumped in a sinkhole near Cave Hill reappeared. The Cave Hill area seemed the best location to search. It was in that hill that the biggest cave in the area was found, and persistant rumors told of hollow-sounding ground and disappearing cattle. He could not coax Andrew to re-explore Ruffner's, the Old Cave. But he might be able to get him to search for an opening in one of the many likely sinks.

The preoccupation with finding "the Cave" was taking more and more of Stebbins' time. His finances, meager to begin with, were so strained that he felt he should move on before all of this precious capital was gone. Amelia did not know how precarious their finances were, but she sensed the growing urgency that Stebbins tried to conceal.

"I'm afraid that we will have to move on," began Stebbins. "If things don't pick up in the next two weeks we might go over to New Market; it doesn't look as if the railroad will be here until next year."

Amelia nodded her agreement. There was no need to discuss it; the little activity in the studio was a constant worry to her. Perhaps it would be better in New Market.

Stebbins changed his advertisement in the *Page Courier* to read:

All who wish pictures will please call before the 15th of next month as I anticipate changing my base of operations.

"You have room for another line, Mr. Stebbins," said T. J. Berrey as he counted out the words in the new ad.

Stebbins took the pencil and with his left hand carefully wrote:

PRODUCE TAKEN IN EXCHANGE FOR WORK DONE

There was not much more he could do; perhaps they could try once more to see if there was a suitable cave under Cave Hill.

# III

July had been unusually hot, with little rain; by the first weeks of August the fields were parched and yellow. Only Billy was in condition for the strenuous work required to search for "the cave." Stebbins, the accepted leader, provided the stimulus for the continued search. His movements were deliberate as he conserved his strength in the heat, but he always encouraged them all to work as if there was something to be found—just ahead.

Andrew continued with the group because he enjoyed exploring caves. There was little work during the summer in the tinsmith shop, so he was able to devote his days to the project. He was a small man, not over five-foot-four, agile, gregarious, optimistic, and pleasant company. He liked and respected Stebbins and let him take the initiative.

Billy, at twenty-six, was strong, energetic, and full of the love of the outdoors. His entire life had been spent in Page County on the farm. An expert hunter and fisherman, he knew the woods and streams of the area, and adapted to the search for the cave with the same enthusiasm he had for a hunt. But when Trent dropped out Billy had to do all the energetic climbing, up steep slopes to check limestone ledges for holes, and down into sinkholes to search for openings. It was exhausting drudgery in the heat. Billy worked without a shirt, pursued by gnats and horse flies as the sweat poured off his back. If he had not coerced his uncle into aiding them, he probably would have quit. Stebbins, aware of this conflict in Billy, knew the discouragement that gripped him. Stebbins had not told the others of his own decision to move on, since this would have caused the entire project to collapse, so he continued as if nothing had happened.

"There just has to be another cave in this hill," he said stubbornly to his companions. "We've checked all the likely spots on the Isaac Williams' land. This morning I spoke to Andrew Broaddus to get permission to look into the holes on the ten-acre tract that he has next to Williams on the south side of Cave Hill."

Andrew was very familiar with the property on Cave Hill, all of it visible from the Sperryville-New Market Turnpikes. To the west was the 16 acres of Isaac Williams, part pasture, part woodlot. Next to it lay the Broaddus property, rocky, thin pasture land dotted with clumps of brush that outlined the cluttered sinkholes. And to the east, nearest town, was the scruffy overgrown land of Saumel Buracker. Stebbins had agreed that the last excursion would be to Buracker's land. But he tempered this with, "I just know there has to be a cave there."

Early in the morning to avoid the extreme heat on August 13, 1878, they were walking by the stone fence that bordered the Broaddus land. The three "Phantom Chasers" were accompanied by James Modisett, Andrew's first cousin, and 13-year-old John "Quint" Campbell, Andrew's nephew.

Halfway up the hill they stopped to survey the land. Stebbins checked his notes for sinks they had already examined.

"How about that sink over there?" asked Billy, pointing east over the fence to a forty-foot-wide opening surrounded by brush.

"I checked that years ago," answered Andrew. "That's on the Buracker property."

"I think I'll look at it," said Billy as he leaped over the fence, parted the bushes, and disappeared into the depression. In a moment he called out from below.

"Andy, come on over and look at this! I can feel some cold air coming out."

Andrew climbed over the fence while the others gathered the equipment and followed. When they got to the hole, both Billy and Andrew were at the far end of a ten-foot-deep pit digging at a pile of leaves beneath a ledge at the north side.

"There's quite a breeze coming out," Andrew repeated. "This looks like it might have some promise."

No one was impressed for Andrew had said that about a dozen such openings. But since the base of the hole was only wide enough for two men to work

comfortably, the others waited patiently as the work progressed.

Stebbins, not wishing to discourage the initiative shown by Billy, cleared some of the brush at the lip of the sink and waited expectantly. Billy passed up some sticks and a log to Quint and James, who threw them aside.

Stebbins removed the hammers and chisels from the bucket, tied a rope to the bail, and lowered it to Billy and Andrew. They filled the bucket using their hands as it was too close to use a shovel, and signaled to Stebbins to heave it up and dump it into the pasture.

"Mr. Stebbins," called Billy excitedly. "You should take a look at this." Stebbins scrambled into the pit. He felt the cold air welling up beneath the loose rubble. There was no doubt that this was a most encouraging sign. But he restrained his comments, fearing that this might be another disappointment.

The men loosened the smaller rocks and tossed them out of the sink. The larger ones required the combined efforts of all so they would not roll back in and crush the men. By three o'clock it was apparent that this was more than "just another sinkhole." They were nearly ten feet down. Cold air rushed out of the entrance in such volume that it was chilling to the skin despite the hot sun. Andrew, looking over Billy's shoulder, said, "I think it is large enough for me to get down into."

He pushed a few small rocks in and saw them bound away out of sight. He thought he heard an echo as the rock thumped into something.

Removal of rotting leaves and sticks exposed wet limestone walls. Through the mulch the breeze brought them the odor of washed potatoes and damp earth. Andrew tried to light a candle, but the breeze blew it out. Holding it unlit in his teeth, he grasped the rope with both hands, backed into the hole, and slid out of sight. He could talk to Billy only a few feet away and described the ledge he was standing on. Now, out of the direct draft of the entrance, he lit his candle.

"I'm going down a little more," he said.

The rope grew taut and a clatter of stones was heard; then the rope went slack.

"Boys, he's let go of the rope!" cried Billy.

"Don't be uneasy," called Andrew, who could still hear Billy. "I'm all right."

Quint, unable to restrain his curiosity, took another candle. Before Billy could stop him, he grasped the rope and scampered into the hole after his uncle.

It was an easy descent for the thirteen-year-old boy. Halfway down the muddy incline his uncle grabbed him and held out his candle so they both could see the room below.

Their lights revealed an astonishing sight. At eye level there were hundreds of carrot-like formations. On the bottom of each pendant was a drop of water. They looked like tiny diamonds in the reflected candle light. At the bottom Andrew stood up, and holding his candle high, attempted to see the extent of the room. It appeared to be more than forty feet in diameter. From below, the ceiling looked like a pin cushion of formations; the walls glistened, and in front of them was a huge, floor-to-ceiling column.

Andrew ordered Quint to stay put. Then he darted behind the formation, and looked into a passage on the left, trying to gauge the extent of the room. In a few moments he returned to Quint, still standing at the foot of the entrance slope. The boy was frightened and glad to have him return.

"Don't you say anything about this, do you hear?" said Andrew with the excitement of the exploration in his voice. "Let's be mum about this until we see what the cave is really like."

Quint again nodded, and followed Andrew up the slope they had just traversed back to the entrance.

"We're coming up," called Andrew, and then, pushing Quint ahead of him, used the rope as an aid. As they climbed out of the tiny entrance, he whispered, "Don't forget, Quint, let's be mum."

The men on the surface were becoming concerned, and Billy was about to come in after them when he heard Andrew's call. Quint said nothing as Billy helped him through the hole. Behind him struggled Andrew.

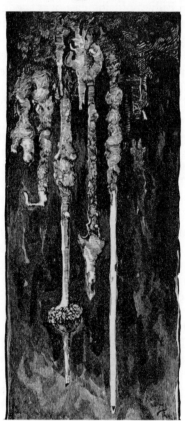

*Down from the ceiling*

All looked expectantly at Andrew, as he caught his breath from the exertions of the exit. He paused and then said, "It ain't nothin' but a damned hole in the ground."

This discouraging report was a crushing blow to Stebbins and Billy. James Modisett, sitting on the lip of the sink, chortled in laughter, but he stopped short when he saw the angry glint in his cousin Andrew's eye.

"Well, it does seem funny that you have been working all day in that 'damned hole in the ground,'" he said defensively.

There was silence as the five gathered up their tools and rope and started along the fence row toward the village. Nobody spoke when James Modisett turned off to his home. When he was out of sight and earshot, Andrew let out an earsplitting rebel yell.

"Yeoohee! We've found it!" he cried. Both Billy and Stebbins thought that he had gone mad. He jumped up and down with excitement shouting, "It's the cave! It's the cave!"

When they finally calmed him down, he told of the brief exploration that he and Quint had made. The two men listened eagerly to the description of the entrance room and the possible extensions still to be explored.

Benton Stebbins now exerted his leadership. "You did the right thing keeping quiet about this," he said to Andrew. Turning to Quint he said, "Don't you mention any of this to anybody, not even your Pa. It's got to be a secret, until we say otherwise." The boy, confused and somewhat frightened by the antics of the men, hastily agreed, and at the first opportunity left for home.

"Why don't we come back here tonight, after dark, and take a good look at the cave before we mention it to anybody else," suggested Stebbins.

"Bring a change of clothes," suggested Andrew. "We may be in the cave all night." The men separated, filled with excitement, and pledged not to tell anyone of the find.

About eight o'clock that night they met back at the sinkhole for their secret excursion. Undressing in the field, they folded and placed their good clothes in a pile at the top of the sink, changing into the old clothes they had been working in all week. By the light of one candle they secured the rope to a small tree and descended into the cave. No one spoke until they reached the bottom of the entrance room.

The combined glow of their candles provided light for them to view the chamber. Stebbins was enthralled. Compared to Ruffner's Cave this was a palace. The white walls reflected tiny lights, as the grotesque shadows added to the feeling of mystery and wildness.

Andrew proudly led them into the left-hand passage. They soon passed the extent of his previous exploration and were looking at sights never seen before by man. Stalactites in profusion hung down over the more massive stalagmites. The comparatively smooth floor required little effort to walk upright through the winding tunnel. Each turn in the passage brought shouts of wonder. After a few hundred yards the passage narrowed; they turned back and gasped again at the myriad sights they had failed to notice on their way in. From the entrance room Andrew turned right to a passage that seemed to descend beneath the entrance slope. A room was filled with tiny colorful straw-like formations that were white, caramel, or even bright red. They couldn't traverse the slippery way without brushing against some of them.

Billy and Stebbins were both confused

as to directions in the cave. Only Andrew, who had explored many caves, kept his sense of direction. When it was time to return the others hesitated, but he boldly and surely led them out.

They went down a slope into a broad corridor with high ceilings. Andrew, still the leader, suddenly splashed into a pool of crystal-clear water. As he jumped back, mud which he had stirred up began to silt up the pool, making visible in the dim light the outline of the water.

The passage narrowed to about six feet. The pool that Andrew had blundered into reached from wall to wall and it looked as if there was no way to continue without swimming or wading. The tiny candles did not penetrate the blackness ahead, but without hesitation Andrew boldly waded into the pool.

"Careful!" admonished Stebbins, but Andrew already was up to his waist. He paused briefly but began to sink into the muddy bottom. With an effort he struggled back to shore.

"We'll need a boat for that," gasped Andrew. The cold water had been an unexpected shock and he was soaked to the waist. Recovering his composure he squatted down on the bank and stared at his candle.

"What are you doing?" asked Stebbins.

"I want to see if there is any breeze coming from up ahead. The air we felt at the entrance had to be coming from a bigger cave than we have seen here," he said. "Be still; don't anybody move."

Silently the three men stared at his candle. The flames bent slightly toward the entrance. Campbell took out another candle and lit it. Then he pinched out one and as it smoldered watched the smoke perceptibly drift down the passage toward the entrance.

"There's more cave ahead," he said, "but we'll have to build a boat for it."

Time had flown swiftly in the excitement and no one realized that three hours had passed since they had entered the cave. The thrill of discovery made them forget their aching muscles, and the hot wax dripping on their hands, but as they returned to the entrance fatigue began to catch up with them.

"Let's not let on about this until we know who owns the land," said Stebbins.

"Sam Buracker owns it, or at least used to. He's been bankrupt for years," responded Andrew. "He's knee-deep in judgments; his son-in-laws have been trying to sell off the land to settle his debts."

"Billy," said Stebbins, "why don't you check at the courthouse tomorrow and find out the situation now?" Since Billy's father was county sheriff it would cause no suspicion if he were to search records or inquire about the land.

It was past midnight when the men, redressed in their street clothes, returned to town. Next evening the trio met in Andrew's tinsmith shop and Billy reported on what he had learned at the courthouse.

"Sam Buracker was a very successful merchant in town before the war," began Billy. For Stebbins' benefit he added, "He lives in the big house at the corner of Main Street and Water Street. He was hit pretty hard after the war; a lot of his customers were on credit, and when they couldn't pay, he took a lot of land in payment of bills. Then he got sick and his business fell off. He seemed to be doing pretty good, but after Daniel Miller brought suit against him it came out that he owed over $15,000 with no way of paying it back. Sam has five daughters, and one son named Eddie. All the girls married well but the family took it pretty hard that all this money was owed by their father. Some creditors got together and brought suit against the estate. One of the son-in-laws, William T. Biedler who is a merchant in Baltimore, came up with a plan he felt would satisfy the claims and still keep the land in the family.

"All of the judgments that Sam had accumulated over the years were turned over to the court to try and collect. H. J. Smoot acted as the attorney. This brought in about $2,000. Then all of the land, over 500 acres, that was in Buracker's name was put up for auction, including the twenty-eight and a half acres on Cave Hill. That was back in June. Most of it was bought by J. B. Sibert, another son-in-law of Buracker. But there were no bids on the Cave Hill property! In July it was brought up again and the only bid for Cave Hill was from Eddie Buracker, Sam's son. He bid eight dollars an acre, and offered a ten per cent down payment on the purchase. The advertisement said twenty per cent down, but according to George Bailey, the auctioneer, he ain't never paid even the twenty-eight dollars down payment!"

"So that's the way it stands now?" asked Stebbins as Billy paused after this involved explanation. "The tract that has the cave has been bought by Ed Buracker at the last sale, but he has not paid the deposit yet?"

"That's right," said Billy, "The terms of all the sales of this land is twenty per cent down, the balance in one, two and three years, equal payments, plus six per cent interest."

Stebbins pondered a while, then said, "Before we go to Ed Buracker about the cave on the land, why don't we wait and see if he makes the down payment. If he does, we'll approach him about selling or becoming a partner. If he don't make the down payment then we'll request that the land be put back on the block

and sold at the next session."

"Sure," said Billy. "That's done lots of times. The buyer can't come up with the money so it is resold. The Snake pasture was resold at the last auction because no money was paid down with the sale and the court threw the bid out."

"It seems to me," said Andrew, "we'd be better off just going to Eddie and buying it from him."

"He's going to think it's mighty strange we want that particular tract," said Stebbins. "Besides, from what Billy tells us, it's not clear that he owns it. Looks like the creditors have more interest in it than he does."

The men thought quietly about this turn of events. Finally Stebbins spoke, "There doesn't seem to be much choice. Nobody seems to have a clear title. Until it goes through the sheriff's sale, we don't know who has the right to sell it. We're just going to have to wait and see. What do you think it will sell for at the auction?" Stebbins turned to Billy for that information.

"Maybe ten dollars an acre, not more than twenty. None of the Buracker land went for more than twenty," he replied.

"That could be as much as $600. We'd need $120 for the down payment. That's forty dollars apiece," mused Stebbins. "Do you have forty dollars?"

He turned to Andrew who shook his head.

"Do you?" he asked Billy, who looked startled.

"Don't feel bad; neither do I!" he laughed. "It looks as if we all couldn't even raise the down payment!"

"The next court day is September tenth. That gives us almost a month to come up with the money," said Billy hopefully. "But I don't know how I could ever make forty dollars less I borrow it from Pa. But I think I'd better have better security than a hole in the ground if I hope to get it from him," he muttered.

"Are we agreed that we wait until the next session of the court and buy it at auction?" asked Stebbins. The other men nodded. Andrew added, "Unless Eddie Buracker pays up his down payment before the next court date."

"Then we will have to try and make an agreement with him about the cave," said Stebbins. "It's important that we have agreements with the surrounding property owners just in case there is another entrance on their land. We'll have to make individual agreements regarding our rights if we discover anything. Since we don't have any money to put up and they own the land, the best we can hope is to share equally in the discovery. But we must have it in writing."

Stebbins went through his coat pocket and pulled out a folded piece of paper. "Here are the names of the five owners of Cave Hill: Sam Buracker, Andrew Broaddus, Isaac Williams, Caroline Flinn and D. E. Almond."

"Is that Dave Almond?" asked Billy. "He has owed Pa a bill for nearly three years. I don't think we'd have any trouble getting an agreement with him."

After more discussion the three men were in agreement. They would search for other entrances and keep quiet about their discovery until after the next court day sale, September 10, 1878. Andrew seemed uncertain, but Stebbins convinced him that it would be difficult or impossible to purchase the property if the secret of the cave were to leak out. It would be necessary to leave the cave sealed and not visit it again until after the sale.

"It ain't going to be easy. I know that cave goes; I can just feel it, that breeze and all," protested Andrew as he recalled the thrill and excitement of the night before.

## IV

When Benton told Amelia of the discovery he knew she would keep the secret, and that it would assure her that they would not be moving soon. But he was concerned with problems of the purchase of the land. When they started the search he thought that he could make the owner a partner, have no personal expenses in acquiring the land, but share in the rewards of the cave. This was fine when there was no cave, but now that there was one, he had doubts about partnerships and joint ownership of the land.

"Those who have nothing, have nothing to risk," Stebbins muttered, not sure that was an actual quotation, but it seemed to apply. The logical business decision would be to move on with his portable studio to more favorable territory. But the discovery of the cave and the possible financial profits complicated matters. He had pledged to his partners he would keep the cave a secret, but he felt he must confide in someone for advice or reassurance. The logical person was Charles Vorhees. After waiting a few days he met with him and told him, "We think we have found a better cave than the one atop Cave Hill, and it looks like it can be bought."

"I don't know anything about caves," said Charles, "but I do know something about land, and that's pretty poor land all right. How much land is there?"

"About twenty-eight and a half acres," replied Stebbins.

"Well, you really have to get it cheap if you want to farm it," advised Charles. "That rocky, thin soil is good for nothin' but pasture and maybe fruit trees."

"I'm not sure that the cave would be a success," mused Stebbins. "We can't wait for fruit trees to grow. I guess we'll just have to see how cheap the land will go before we decide what to do with it."

"Can you take me to see it?" asked Charles. "Even though I don't care much for caves, I'd like to see what you've found."

"We've covered up the entrance with rocks," said Stebbins. "Nobody can see it until we decide whether we can buy it at the auction next month."

"How do you expect to pay for it?" asked Charles, who knew his brother-in-law's financial situation. "I'm sorry that I won't be able to help you; I've made an offer to Sam Judd to buy into his carriage business. That will take all I have, and then some."

"Well, I certainly wish you luck in

that venture, Charles," said Stebbins. "Our scheme won't take much money to start, maybe forty dollars each, but it might as well be a thousand when you don't have it."

Stebbins had no spare cash in his business; in fact, he had only enough money for two weeks' rent. Unless he found more photographic work the family would have problems eating, to say nothing of providing a down payment on a cave. Fortunately as the end of summer approached the farmers would be in town with their produce. There would be some money around, but not much since harvest time was also a barter time. Livestock and produce changed hands; but hard money was scarce. Forty dollars was a lot to raise in a short time.

There was nothing that he could easily sell. They had sold all of their odds and ends when they left Maryland. The equipment for the photographic business did not have a ready sale. Besides these were the tools of the trade and he could not risk the loss of his livelihood.

One item might provide the necessary cash, but he would have to talk to Amelia about it. "It doesn't look as if I'm going to be able to come up with the money necessary to make a deposit on the land," Stebbins said to her. "Charles says he is going in with Sam Judd in the carriage business and he don't have the money to lend me."

Amelia said nothing immediately. It was difficult for her to consider seriously investing in property for the purpose of opening a cave. Her husband's project had not captivated her from the beginning, and the extra burden his frequent absences put on her left her tired and irritable. She was lonely here in Luray. She was not accepted very quickly by the townsfolk. Her accent was clearly northern. While she had a pleas-

ant and friendly demeanor, no friendships had been offered her.

Setting up the studio and house, and tending to Eugene had kept her busy enough at first so lack of companionship did not seem important. But with Benton out tramping over the countryside lately and digging holes in the ground, she began to feel isolated.

"Charles thinks there is an opportunity in the harness business," she finally said. "It does seem to be a more likely place to put his money." She hesitated, unwilling to continue as she felt that she might hurt her husband's feelings. But after a pause, the stress of the past few weeks urged her to continue.

"It's a crazy thing to invest in!" she blurted out. "A cave, of all things. What do you know about caves?"

Stebbins was startled at her vehemence. It was not customary for her to be so verbal and give her opinion about business decisions. It never occurred to him to ask her advice about the search for the cave, and, now that a cave had been found, he never thought she might have an opinion about investing in it.

"Everybody in town thinks you and the Campbells are a little touched," she continued. "They call you the 'Phantom Chasers' and worse. It has been hard for me to make friends in town. I can hear the sniggers, and see the smiles when they talk about you and that search for the great cave."

"But Amelia," responded Stebbins. "We have found it—or think we have! It's the best opportunity we have ever had. When the trains come through, there will be hundreds of people who will pay to go to the cave—and pay a half a dollar admission too. If we can only buy it before it gets out that the cave is there, we will be rich." Stebbins was now also warming up to his favorite subject and he plunged ahead.

"The sale will take place on September tenth. Each of us has to put up forty dollars for the down payment." Stebbins paused, choosing his words carefully. "I thought we might be able to borrow fifty dollars on your Mason and Hamlin organ. Mrs. Duncan has said she took a strong liking to it."

Stebbins glanced up to look at Amelia, and realized he had made a mistake. The mention of the organ had taken the fire from her eyes that was replaced by a hurt expression. "You wouldn't sell that, would you?" she asked.

"Not sell it," Stebbins replied more gently, "only borrow on it until we can get some return from the cave." The discussion of her mother's organ had reminded Amelia of the tragic loss of her parents only a few months ago.

"We'll try and find the money someplace else," he said, putting his arm around her.

Andrew Campbell was also having a difficult time. The New Era tinsmith shop had taken all his capital. He owed money on supplies and he had money due him that could not be collected until the harvest. The most he could spare was about ten dollars cash. Although not the most astute businessman, he was a good mechanic and a likeable fellow, but considered the dreamer of the three Campbell boys.

Andrew knew that he would not be able to borrow from his brother, the sheriff, for that was Billy's territory. He went to A. W. McKim, the druggist, one of the most successful businessmen in town.

"A. W.," he started, "I've got a problem. Seems like I'm going to need some money for a few days, and maybe you could lend it to me."

McKim, who could be the friendliest of men, stiffened a little with this, and said, "What kind of money, Andy?"

"Oh thirty, or thirty-five dollars," he replied casually.

McKim whistled softly. "That's a lot of money. What do you need it for?"

"Well, it's kind of personal," replied Andrew faltering a little. He knew that the request was going to require more information about the project than he was prepared to give.

"Have you got any security," McKim asked. "Have you tried the bank?"

"No," answered Andrew slowly. "It only has to be for a short time. I didn't want to go through all of that for only thirty dollars."

"Things are tight now," answered McKim. "If you can wait until the harvest, maybe then I can help you."

"That'll be too late," muttered Andrew. "Thanks, anyway."

The rejection, although offered kindly, stung Andrew. Of all three men, he was the most excited about the cave discovery. It was difficult for him to keep the secret. He also knew that it was going to be difficult if not impossible for him to borrow the money unless he offered some reason for the loan.

Andrew's next attempt to obtain money was from Dr. David H. Brumback. He found the doctor in his garden. After a few minutes conversation Andrew asked "Are you a Mason?"

"Of course I am; you know that."

"Can you keep this conversation confidential?"

"Certainly, if you want to," replied the doctor.

"I'm afraid I'm going to bust if I don't tell somebody!" Andrew said excitedly, and he tumbled out the story of the discovery. While a great relief to Andrew, this revelation was not so exciting to Brumback. When Andrew finished, the doctor waited. Finally he said, "That's wonderful, Andrew, but why is it a secret?''

Andrew quickly explained the legal status of the property, concluding with ''and if Eddie Buracker don't come up with the money before the tenth, it will be auctioned off again.''

Dr. Brumback clearly understood the situation the men were in, but he did not see any difficulty in purchasing the land.

''That land is not worth ten dollars an acre,'' he said. ''You can buy the whole hill for fifteen dollars an acre, and get change to boot.''

''But that's the problem; we don't have the money,'' said Andrew. ''If we tell about the discovery of the cave, the price will go up and we couldn't touch it. In fact, we don't even have the deposit money if we buy it at auction.''

''I see your problem,'' mused the doctor. ''How can I help you?''

''You could loan me thirty dollars,'' answered Andrew with a grin.

The doctor roared with laughter and slapped Andrew on the back. ''I'll loan you thirty dollars, but I don't want to know anything about this auction business. As a Lodge brother I couldn't do any less for you,'' he said. ''But I would like to see the cave when you get this straightened out.''

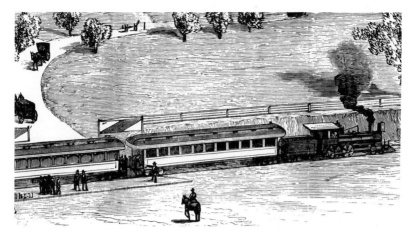

## V

Tuesday, September 10, 1878 was circuit court day at Page County Court House in Luray. There was a full docket this month because the August term had been skipped, and many cases had been held over from July, as well as new cases scheduled. Lawyers from all over the county were in town. The Washington House and the Rust House were full, and the normal summer pace was speeded up.

First item was court-ordered sales of properties. George Bailey, Clerk of the Court, would auction them off in the tradition of old English law. Handbills had been distributed and posted in the public places around the county. These pink, blue and buff handbills were printed by the *Page-Courier* and put up by Captain Richard S. Parks as the Sergeant of the Court. Unfortunately Captain Parks neglected to list "Cave Hill" property with the printed order and so he had handwritten on the fifty sheets:

CAVE HILL, 28-1/2 ACRES OF LAND

This was not missed by Benton Stebbins, who hoped Eddie Buracker would not step forward during the ten days prior to the sale and pay the deposit for the tract.

Stebbins, Andrew, and Billy waited for the proceedings, to be held outside the court house, to begin. Sheriff William Campbell joined them under the court house portico.

"It doesn't look as if Eddie will be here," said the sheriff. "I talked to Dr. Smoot who is handling the sale for the creditors and he said that he spoke to Jim Weaver about putting the property back on the docket. Jim said he was authorized to speak for Eddie and that we should put it up for sale."

The others smiled at that news. Billy was unable to get the money for the deposit, unless he borrowed it from his father. He had informed the sheriff of the discovery and, with the agreement of the others, William Campbell planned to take the place of his son in the partnership. It was agreed that he would do the actual bidding in the name of the group: William Campbell, Andrew J. Campbell, and Benton Stebbins. This seemed reasonable, since Stebbins was a stranger and felt that the sheriff would know better than the others the mechanics of the purchase.

"By the order of the Court of Page County, Virginia, The Honorable Mark Bird, presiding, the following properties will be sold to the highest bidder."

Finally George Bailey rapped on the

*Page County Court House, Luray, Virginia. Built in 1833.*

door of the Court House to get the attention of the twenty or thirty people gathered; the murmur of conversation ceased as Bailey read from the printed handbill a description of the first property.

Stebbins and Andrew started to move closer to the auctioneer, but the sheriff held up his hand and whispered, "No rush; the Cave Hill property will be the last on the list."

There was little enthusiasm in the early bidding. Times in the valley were hard; no one had much money to invest. Only those who could actually work the land were serious bidders.

It was common for properties to be auctioned to a bidder who was unable to come up with the deposit money. Bids would go up by portions of a dollar per acre, with the auctioneer calling "ten cents more. Am I bid ten cents more?"

Bailey, an experienced auctioneer, lapsed into the sing-song chant of the profession, trying to stir up interest. The first property, the Snapp tract, had been sold before on June 27, 1878, 106 acres at $8.80 per acre. It was being rebid now with a starting bid of $8.79 per acre because of a default in payment. After a few halting starts the tract was sold for $8.90 per acre to Nebraska D. Hite.

The next property, 150 acres, went to J. B. Hudson for $17.50 per acre. This was fine bottom land on the west side of the Hawksbill River, and was considered a good purchase by the onlookers at the auction. Sales began to move more swiftly and Bailey started sweating as the sun heated the courtyard. There was no wind and the drone of the auctioneer could be heard clearly by the four men waiting at the edge of the porch for the Cave Hill property.

Finally all parcels printed on the sheet were sold. Bailey read from the bottom the addition that Captain Parks had added.

"The next property in—I can't make out the words—can you help me, Captain?"

"Cave Hill—twenty-eight and a half acres of land," called Captain Parks.

"Right. Terms, one-fifth with purchase, the balance in one, two, and three year equal payments, plus interest.

What am I bid?'' Bailey asked the group.

Sheriff William Campbell moved closer to the wood crate that the auctioneer was standing on and called out, ''Nine dollars!''

''I have nine dollars. Who'll bid two bits more? Two bits more?''

James C. Weaver raised his hand to catch Bailey's attention.

''I have a quarter more. Will you raise it to nine-and-a-half?'' he chanted as he looked around for other bidders. There were none except for the Sheriff who nodded.

''Now I have nine-and-a-half. Will you make it two bits more?'' he glanced over at Jim Weaver who nodded his head.

Before the auctioneer could make his next call, William Campbell raised his hand and said, ''Eleven dollars.''

There was a murmur from the spectators but Bailey was not taken by surprise. He shouted, ''I have eleven dollars, will you make it twelve?'' looking at the only other bidder, Jim Weaver. Weaver hesitated a moment, looked quizzically at Campbell, then slowly said, ''And a quarter.''

''I have eleven-and-a-quarter; will you make it a half?''

''Twelve dollars,'' said Campbell.

There was a buzz among the onlookers. This property was well known in town. It had been in the Buracker family for many years. It was poor, rocky land with thin soil, pocked with sinkholes and brier patches. It wasn't worth much more than ten dollars per acre. Twelve dollars seemed to be a top price.

''And two bits,'' came a dogged response from Jim Weaver.

''I have twelve-and-a-quarter. What will you bid?'' said Bailey looking at William Campbell.

''Thirteen dollars,'' he said firmly.

The heat of the day was forgotten. Here was some excitement for the crowd. Everyone listened keenly. Billy, Andrew and Stebbins were looking around nervously and wondering why Jim Weaver was bidding up the property.

''He might be bidding for Isaac Williams,'' whispered Andrew to Stebbins. Williams owned about eighteen acres on Cave Hill, and might be interested in the adjoining piece.

Bailey was now continuing his call and repeating it as he looked directly at Jim Weaver. With a visible effort and a little discomfort, Weaver said, ''And a quarter.''

''Fourteen dollars,'' Campbell clearly called out.

Weaver was puzzled now. He had been advised by S. A. Buracker to approve the rebidding. But Buracker's son-in-law, W. T. Biedler, who was in Baltimore and unable to attend the sale, told him not to go more than twelve or thirteen dollars. The determination and positive action by the sheriff was more than he could understand.

''And ten cents,'' he responded to the auctioneer's call.

''Fifteen dollars,'' the response rang out.

Now his curiosity was aroused. This was not a valuable piece of land. It was only twenty-eight and a half acres. Every additional dollar bid raised the total amount due by $28.50. He could not figure why the sheriff was so insistent with his bidding.

''And ten cents,'' he continued.

There were loud noises from the crowd now that the bidding took on the appearance of a contest. Everyone was getting vicarious pleasure from the competition.

''Sixteen dollars,'' William Campbell

said steadily.

It suddenly seemed warm to Jim Weaver. He was not going to be pushed into this, but he wanted to see if the determination of the sheriff would continue. So he replied, "And a dime."

There was a gasp from the crowd; Jim Weaver suddenly realized what he had done. He glanced fearfully at William Campbell who returned the look steadily. At the auctioneer's call the sheriff casually said, "Seventeen dollars."

Jim Weaver breathed a sigh of relief, shook his head at the auctioneer's call, and looked away.

"Going, going, gone. Sold to—" Bailey leaned over to William Campbell who whispered to him—". . . William Campbell, Andrew J. Campbell, and B. P. Stebbins for the sum of seventeen dollars per acre.

"That concludes the bidding. The purchasers will see the clerk for the payment of the deposits in ten minutes in the clerk's office."

Bailey stepped off his box, gathered together his papers, and went into the courthouse. The group outside was still buzzing about the last sale. It presented the only excitement of the day, and when they realized the land was bought by the "Phantom Chasers," some of the townsfolk thought it was pretty funny. It certainly was not a good purchase in the minds of the men who made their living from the soil and knew the market value of tillable land.

"You going to move your tin shop out there?" one of the men asked Andrew.

Andrew was too excited to answer. He only smiled and nodded as the laughter ripplied through the crowd. He was bursting to tell about the cave, but a stern glance from his brother kept him silent.

"Have you got your money?" the sheriff asked his brother and Stebbins. They nodded, elated over the events of the auction, and went into the courthouse to see the clerk.

Stebbins was excited, but was facing an action that bothered him. He had promised Amelia that he would not sell the Mason and Hamlin organ. But as the time for the sale drew near there appeared to be no other way to get the money. Using the organ as security, he had obtained a loan of fifty dollars from Mrs. Duncan. Now the money must be spent, but he silently pledged that he would make this a successful venture. Stebbins had never hurt Amelia like this before, and her attachment to the instrument caused him guilt feelings. He must try to have her understand. The hurt look in her eyes haunted him still.

H. J. Smoot was in the clerk's office. As attorney for the creditors of S. A. Buracker, he was one of the commissioners of sale of the real estate and had to authorize the transfer of the property.

"There was an error in the terms of the sale," said Dr. Smoot. "No, no, nothing to worry about; it is in your favor. The original order of the court specified that the terms would be 'Enough of the purchase money to be paid in cash to pay the costs of the suit and the charges attending said sale.' That would be closer to 15 percent of the purchase price."

The men looked at each other. The total sale price was almost five hundred dollars. Then the sheriff remarked, "Well, we have the money for the one fifth down, we might as well pay it now and save the interest on the balance."

"All right," said Dr. Smoot writing out the cost of the sale. "That will be $96.90. The balance will be in three equal payments, plus six percent interest—let's see—that will be $136.95 per year."

Benton Stebbins and Andrew Campbell gave their money to William Campbell, and adding his portion, he paid it to the clerk of the court.

"Now do we own it?" asked Billy.

"No, not yet," said Dr. Smoot, "We have to get the approval of the commissioners and the court before we can close the sale."

"How long will that take?" asked Andrew impatiently.

"It should be completed at this session of the circuit court," said Dr. Smoot. "But that is just a formality. Since the commissioners are all here at this session, we can get them to sign this tomorrow."

The three men left the courthouse while the sheriff stayed to sign some of the papers required by the sale. Billy and Andrew wanted to go out that afternoon and dig open the cave.

"Hold on," said Stebbins. "We can't let on about this until all is settled in court. We don't want to go near that cave until we have the commissioner's sale and bonds in hand."

"Well, I guess we can wait a few more days," said Andrew. "But it ain't going to be easy!"

The next few days were difficult for the "Phantom Chasers" as rumors began that the land was more than "just a place to grow fruit trees," as Stebbins was admitting. Jim Weaver spoke to William Campbell and said that he had been authorized to bid by Sam Buracker.

"I just bid it up a bit 'cause you looked so keen on buying it."

The sheriff did not reveal the secret. Four days later on September 14th, the contract bonds were signed, and Billy, Andrew, and Stebbins went out to the property to reopen the cave.

## VI

The candle's thin flame burned like a horizontal finger pointing into the cave.

"The air's blowing in!" called Andrew from the bottom of the sink. The other men stood on the surface and stared down at the flickering flame and Andrew's upturned smiling face. Benton Stebbins, Billy Campbell, Jim Modisett, and Dr. David Brumback worked all afternoon to clear out the choke that had been kicked into the pit by the discoverers a month before.

"It was blowing like the devil when we first discovered it," continued Andrew. "There's got to be a lot of cave somewhere in there."

Tension was building in the minds of the discoverers. They had thought of little else during the past four weeks. Now that the secret of the cave no longer needed to be kept they were anxious to see if it was all they imagined.

The sun was setting as Andrew led the way into the entrance. Stebbins secured a rope to a stump on the surface to use as a hand line. One by one they cautiously descended into the sink, mindful that another slide could undo all of their work. In a few minutes all five stood in the entrance room.

"Yoehee!" shouted Jim Modisett with a rebel yell, the echoes reverberating through the room. "This ain't no mud hole! I thought you said it was nothin' but a damned hole in the ground!"

"Well it is," replied Andrew. "It's the damnedest hole I ever saw."

They were surrounded by a world of strange forms, glistening and sparkling in the flickering candlelight. The only sounds were the utterances of the men and soft drip of water from some formations.

Billy and Andrew were eager to be off, leading the way into the left hand passage. The others followed in single file. With mouth agape Jim stumbled over the rough places, trying to keep up with Andrew and Billy. Dr. Brumback proceeded cautiously, pausing to examine some of the formations closely and feeling them as if to satisfy himself that they were really stone. Benton Stebbins had difficulty controlling his excitement. He lingered behind and tried to study the whole cave by the flickering light of those ahead. Shadows and reflections gave animation to the multitudes of formations. He caught flashes of light and snatches of the voices of his companions ahead of him. The pristine whiteness of some of the stone draperies stood out in brilliant contrast to the onyx colored walls. Stebbins suddenly shook off his reverie, and hastened to catch up with the others.

Andrew was still leading. The way was familiar to him. He had thought of this passage for nearly a month. Each time Billy would catch up with him he would dart ahead to the next room. The group stretched out, each finding his way and pursuing his own individual thoughts. In a few minutes Andrew could go no farther. He came to a low area, got down on his hands and knees, and then on his stomach holding the candle ahead to light his way. Only his feet were visible to Billy, crouched behind him.

Andrew struggled out of the narrow passage and sat on the floor next to Billy as the others joined them

"I remember this passage as being longer," said Andrew. "Seems like there was more cave than this."

"Let's go back and check out all the side passages," offered Billy as he started back. Dr. Brumback and Stebbins had only a brief glance at the last room before they too turned and retraced their steps.

The search revealed only one more room than they had seen on their first trip. This was jammed with hundreds of sodastraw-like stalactites, and curious twisted and bulbous stalactites and stalagmites. Stebbins thought it looked like a geologist's cabinet filled with exotic formations. Near the entrance room Andrew asked his companions to wait while he explored a crevice. He came back, puffing and streaked with mud, muttering that there were four small rooms down there.

"Sort of a basement, but they don't go anywhere and don't amount to much," he reported.

Within an hour they had exhausted the possibilities of the left hand passage and the entrance room. The only area not visited was in the direction of the muddy lake. Andrew was somewhat subdued. He had hoped that he would be able to extend his previous explorations. The swiftness with which they had reached the end, and the lack of other passages made him apprehensive that perhaps this wasn't the great cave he had hoped. He turned his attention to the muddy lake, and as the others followed, he paused at the water's edge.

"Jim," he said to Modisett who was right behind him. "Do you still have that little punt we used on the river last year?"

"Yeah, but it leaks a little."

"Can we borrow it?"

"Sure, but it will never come through that little entrance."

"We'll just have to make a big entrance, then," said Andrew, his good spirits returning. After a few more minutes, the party returned to the entrance, still excited over the prospect of more cave beyond the muddy lake.

"What do you think of it, Doctor?" asked Stebbins when they were all above ground.

"Well, it's mighty pretty, but it's not very big." He realized that this was a discouraging opinion for the three who were investing in the enterprise, so he added, "But there might be more cave beyond the lake."

The rope and tools were gathered up and the men started toward town. As Modisett started off toward his home, Andrew reminded him he'd be over for the boat in the morning

Since no one else in town had been informed of the discovery, the sight of the "Phantom chasers" off to do more excavation the next day, Sunday, created no excitement. By early afternoon the entrance was enlarged enough to admit the boat. Secured by a line to the surface, Billy, Andrew, and Quint helped guide the huge object down the entrance slope to the cave below. From there they carried the clumsy boat, like pallbearers, to the muddly lake. Stebbins held candles high to light the way. They placed the boat on the steeply sloped bank, and slid it silently into the pool.

From the bank, the way ahead appeared to be clear. The narrow passage had sheer walls for thirty feet with two openings at the end, one above the other. The upper one was oval in shape and decorated with formations. The other was a low arch, only a few feet above the water. But there appeared to be sufficient headroom for the boat to pass beneath into the inviting blackness beyond.

Billy and Andrew clambered into the boat as Stebbins, Quint, and Jim Modisett waited. The two pushed against the walls to propel themselves; the boat serenely drifted toward the black opening ahead. Both crouched low, and, as they approached the overhang, they had to stretch out on their backs, gliding under the obstruction by handholds on the ceiling.

"It's a natural bridge!" called Andrew. This became apparent to those behind as the candles lit up the upper opening and provided a window-like view of more passage beyond. He added, "There's a place to get ashore and it looks as if it goes on. Billy will bring you the boat. There's room for all of us."

This news cheered the party and in a few minutes the rest were ferried to the landing beyond the bridge. Andrew waited at the top of a steep mud slope, flushed from exertion. He had scouted ahead and now knew that his prediction

of a "big cave" was correct. His voice echoed as he urged them to hurry. With the boat pulled ashore, the others hastened to follow, their candles making a bobbing procession as they scrambled up the slippery slope. As the walls widened, only the low ceiling above and the untrodden mud below were visible in their tiny lights. They had entered a huge horizontal crevice, limitless as far as their lights could reveal. Only a few pillars appeared to support the roof. The ceiling was smooth, with meandering cracks outlined with strawlike formations which hung like threads into the room.

"Come over here!" called Andrew, still ahead of the group. When they arrived he was standing on the brink of a canyon that seemed bottomless at first glance. It loomed up forty feet or more to a ceiling that was nearly obscured by thousands of formations. Jim shrank back from the pit, but the others stared in awe at the size of the chamber. It extended as far as their lights could reach in both directions. On the opposite wall of the chasm was a near-vertical wall of huge, white, orange, and red onyx draperies that reflected the light.

Andrew, shaking with excitement, took another candle from his pocket, lit it, and stuck it in the mud. Leaving it there as a beacon, he began to work his way along the chasm, gingerly checking his footholds as he proceeded. The others followed as carefully.

It appeared as if they had stumbled upon another world. Everything was of gigantic size; the lights ahead seemed to be suspended in darkness. The thrill they had felt in the left-hand passage could not be compared with what they felt upon seeing the grandeur of this place. The room was wet and shining with hundreds of tiny pools of crystal-clear water. The dripping stalactites caused

*The Sentinel and the Spectre*

*Above: Imperial Spring     Below: Totem Pole*

*Ballroom*

expanding ripples in the pools that made the candlelight subdued and mysterious. The huge size of the columns and draperies was like nothing they had ever seen. For more than two hours they climbed about in this silent cathedral lost in excitement and appreciation of the beauty.

Finally, even this most spectacular discovery was falling on dulled senses. Andrew's foresight in placing a lighted candle at the point they had entered the room guided them back to the trail where they had left the boat. They were not able to comprehend the full magnitude of their findings; and as they wearily climbed out of the boat and up the slope to the entrance, the full realization of the cave's potential and economic value was several hours away.

The secret was out. It was no longer possible to keep to themselves the knowledge of their discovery. The word spread through town, and the participants were questioned about the wonders they had seen. Stebbins was uneasy about this announcement because he felt they should make the entrance more secure before they made the news public. It was no use. Word reached the *Page-Courier*, and that week there was a note, somewhat tongue-in-cheek, about the sudden rise in the property values of "Cave Hill." This had a personal interest to Andrew Broaddus for he owned the land not twenty feet from the entrance to the cave.

William Campbell Sr. had not yet seen the cave. He was out of town on business after the papers had been signed. They showed him the section of the cave they had already explored, and he too was swept up in the enthusiasm.

Neither Andrew nor Stebbins had any

*On the banks of the Rhine*

money. All of their cash was tied up in the deposit on the land. William Campbell agreed to lend the money for the initial opening of the cave. He felt assured there would be no difficulty in getting financing from the bank, once the cave was viewed and exhibited.

Within a week they enlarged the entrance enough to permit access by men and equipment to do the work necessary to receive visitors. There was no shortage of help. The harvest was nearing an end and the few men required to do the more skillful jobs were available. A car-penter and mason could be obtained for seventy-five cents a day and a laborer for twenty-five cents. In spite of his injured hand Stebbins was an experienced carpenter. He directed work around the entrance, the building of a toolshed on the surface, the masonry stairway, and the wooden door and lintel that permitted controlled access to the cave. Billy and Andrew worked inside building bridges, leveling floors, and constructing handrails as needed.

The first few days were hectic as friends and acquaintances appeared at the entrance wanting a guided tour. Billy and Andrew were eager to stop their work to show off the cave. They even permitted the visitors to help themselves to pieces of a formation that they could break off in the little passage to the left

*The Cathedral*

of the entrance. This area, named Specimen Hall, was quickly vandalized.
When Benton Stebbins became aware of
the depredation he quickly stopped it.
He also insisted upon an admission
charge of fifty cents per person. This
immediately slowed the flow of visitors
and idle curiosity seekers who were
asked to wait until the improvements
were completed so they could see the
cave at its best advantage.

Andrew Broaddus, an exception to
the visitors rule, was conducted on a
complete tour. Broaddus' account in the
October third issue in the *Page-Courier*
was a glowing account with the headline
full of typographical mistakes:

---

## A Wonderful Cave

Subterraneum Vaults of Mammoth
Dimensions!

**Only one mile from Luray.**

COLUMNS AND PILLARS OF STA-
LACTITE AND MARBLE-LIKE
WHITENESS

**MARVELLQUSLY BEAUTIFUL!
INDESCRIBABLY GRAND!**

*CHRYSTAL SPRINGS AND SILVERY
LAKES!*

---

The article gave a lavish description of
the cave, ending with the statement that
the "proprietors are now at work with a
good force preparing for an early illumination."

The article spread the news all over
the valley. In spite of the typographical
errors in the headlines, it was the news
story of the year for Luray. The next
week a correction was printed by T. R.
Berrey.

The types made us say last week "sub-
teraneum" for subterranean; also
"chrystal" for crystal. These types are
devilish queer things; they some times
make saints of things that should be
devils.

Meanwhile there were new discoveries
being made in the cave. Andrew
Campbell could not resist pushing
farther. He would work all day near the
entrance, then, after supper return to
explore deeper into the cave.

He ventured down to the bottom of
one of the deep chasms. Using a rope as a
hand line, and watching his footholds
carefully, he reached the bottom, about
fifty feet down. There he was startled to
find a human skeleton in a partial
kneeling position imbedded in calcite on
the floor. This crumpled object, clearly
of great antiquity, glistened white and
shining from the water that had dripped
on the bleached bones.

This was the first evidence that there
had been any previous human entrance.
When Andrew first entered the cave the
floor showed animal tracks and drop-
pings, but no human footprints. Until
now they were sure they were the first
human visitors, but here, fifteen hundred
feet from the natural entrance, was
positive evidence that the cave had been
discovered—one more mystery that
increased people's interest in seeing this
remarkable cavern.

One reader of the *Page-Courier* account was Major Alexander J. Brand
Jr., the son-in-law of Judge James
Stewart, of Page County Court. Major
Brand served in the Union Forces with
the Pennsylvania Volunteers and parti-
cipated with distinction in the Second
Battle of Bull Run. He started a tea
importing business after the war and tra-

velled throughout the south. Visiting Luray on several occasions on business, he met and married Judge Stewart's daughter, Elizabeth, and presently lived in Philadelphia.

As a part-time correspondent to the *New York Herald* and a friend of Gordon Bennett, its publisher, Major Brand felt it would be of interest to see the cave. If it was as grand as described it would make a good story.

With Judge Stewart, Mrs. Brand, and the Judge's other daughter, Nettie, the Major took a carriage to the cave. From the highway a muddy road led to a level area about fifty feet from the sinkhole. Piles of lumber were stacked in the field nearby.

The visitors were met by Benton Stebbins who was supervising construction of a shelter over the entrance.

"Good afternoon, Judge," said Stebbins extending his left hand to greet him.

"You know my daughters, Mr. Stebbins. I'd like you to meet my son-in-law, Major Brand."

Stebbins bowed to the ladies, and turned to the dapper Major, dressed in a grey flannel suit with velvet lapels. He received an energetic handshake.

"Alex is a correspondent for the *New York Herald*," the Judge said, "and would like to write an article."

"Well, we're not ready for visitors yet, but we'll show you what we can. I'll have Andrew or Billy go with you; they're working in the entrance room."

The brush that had surrounded the lip of the forty-foot sinkhole had been cut and burned. A masonry retaining wall had been built on each side of the crevice and there was now a four-foot-wide stairwell extending to an entrance door. Stebbins provided them with tin reflectors, made by Andrew in his tinsmith shop, that would hold three

*Looking toward the entrance*

candles each.

Stebbins started down the steep steps. The ladies followed close behind, holding their skirts to prevent them from dragging along the masonry walls. The wooden door was ajar and the light from the entrance showed the steps continuing down into the darkness. Pausing, Stebbins lit the candles.

"Be careful of the steps," he said. "The handrails are not complete on the right side."

Andrew Campbell, who was acquainted with Judge Stewart and his family, met them at the bottom. Stebbins left them with Andrew and returned to the work outside.

Andrew told of the discovery of the cave; then when the group became accustomed to the dark, he led them into the left hand passage, pointing out the features recently discovered. Judge Stewart, agile for his years, had no trouble skirting the debris piled along the trail and avoiding the hazards not yet removed for the traffic of tourists. Elizabeth and Nettie went along in good spirits until they came to the narrow wood bridge across Crystal Lake. Apprehensive, they decided to return to the entrance room and wait for the others. The Major, captivated with the formations, offered several suggestions for names. The Napoleon Bust required some imagination and proper lighting to discern, but Andrew felt that if that's what Napoleon looked like, it was a good likeness.

The ladies, after waiting at the large formation in the entrance room, agreed after some urging by the Major to take the short boat ride over Muddy Lake to see the rest of the cave. There was some

giggling and deft handling of skirts by the two sisters, but they were finally safely over the water, climbing up the wooden stairway that had been placed at the end of the pool. The trail had been trenched so that it was no longer necessary to duck when passing from Muddy Lake to the Chasm. But there the work stopped, and the route taken by Judge Stewart, Major Brand, and the two ladies was over the same trail blazed only a few weeks before by the original discoverers. The experience was so exciting that they soon lost concern about the mud or inconvenience. They returned to the entrance filled with the same sense of awe that the others had felt.

"Congratulations!" said Major Brand to Benton Stebbins as they exited. "It's a magnificent cave. The most beautiful I've ever seen."

Stebbins, flushed with the pride of

*Entrance Hall*

*The inconvenience of the trail did not diminish the enjoyment of the Double Column.*

ownership, beamed. The Major continued, "I've seen Weyer's Cave, and trying to compare your cave to Weyer's Cave would be like comparing New York City to the town of Luray." This simile was greeted with laughter and the good humor of the whole experience was shared by the Judge and the ladies.

"We are returning to Philadelphia tomorrow," continued Major Brand, "otherwise I would like to come back to see more. I will send a report to the *New York Herald*. I hope I can influence Mr. Bennett and have it published."

It was an exuberant group that got into the carriage. No one seemed to mind the mud on the cushions and the stains on the hems of the dresses as they clattered off toward town.

Stebbins watched them leave and thought of the railroad. The distance to the Sperryville-New Market pike was less than three hundred yards, and the bumpy drive that had been hastily cleared presented no obstacle to the wagon. Once on the highway it was less than a mile to the center of town and the roadbed of the new, yet-to-be-built railroad. It would still be many months before there would be train service to Luray, so all the visitors that came from out of state would have to come by way of New Market. This would mean a three-hour stage ride over Massanutten Ridge, a distance of more than eleven miles.

To Stebbins, this muddy, debris-piled field held the promise of the success he had always dreamed of. As he turned back to work on the entrance he visualized the day when this spot would be the destination for thousands of people each year. Beneath this ordinary hillside lay the most remarkable discovery he had ever imagined. All the problems, both on the surface and beneath the ground seemed to be easily surmountable now that his dream had come true.

# VII

"We made the New York papers," said Gil Zirkle as he tossed a bundle on the porch of Washington House. The Fast Line from New Market had pulled into town with several passengers. While the stable boy was taking the stage to the barn behind the hotel, Gil cut the string on the newspapers and turned to page three where a headline declared:

WONDERFUL CAVERNS
The Discovery of an Immense Subterranean Palace of Stalacta in Virginia
Developing a Rabbit Hole
Remarkable Natural Formations in the Various Chambers

The article described in glowing terms the discovery of the cave, the huge rooms, and the spectacular formations.

D. T. Young, recent proprietor of Washington House, joined the others on the porch who had gathered to get the mail and news from the stage.

"Major Brand has put us on the map," stated Mr. Young. "It looks as if everybody will see the cave before we do."

This encouraging news was greeted with enthusiasm by all present, and it was not long before everyone in town was aware of the publicity.

Stebbins and Andrew read the story avidly. This was the type of publicity they would need if they were to make a success of the cave, but there was still a great amount of work to be done before regular visitation could take place.

"I'm glad we put a secure lock on the door," said Stebbins. "A lot of damage could be done if just anybody went into the cave, or worse, someone could get hurt. We should schedule a special showing of the cave, an Illumination where townspeople will have the opportunity of seeing its beauties lighted bright as day—just like the bandstand on Saturday night."

"That would take a thousand candles!" said Andrew.

"Maybe more," replied Stebbins. "When do you think we can be ready for a showing?"

"Well, I figure it will take at least two weeks to complete the trails to the Giant's Hall and get the lights set up for the Illumination."

"How about November sixth?" asked Stebbins. "We'll need to put announcements and advertisements in the paper if we hope to get a good crowd."

With the deadline agreed upon, the work continued at an increased pace. Additional exploration was suspended

*Above: The Camel's Head    Below: Entrance to the Ballroom*

and all efforts were focused upon the opening and the illumination of all the rooms.

Stebbins was now working in the cave with the others. The outside work was completed and the entrance stairway was fitted with a safe handrail. Lumber, rough sawed and green from the mill, had been selected for the steps and platforms. Only the handrails had been planed and smoothed. It was felt that the rough lumber would stand up best in the humid atmosphere. The odor of the oak was pungent as the curing wood was exposed to the cave's constant temperature.

Muddy Lake presented a problem. Andrew had probed into the silt in the bottom with a pole to see if a platform or bridge might be built to replace the boat. But one morning they found that Muddy Lake had completely disappeared! Nearly six feet of water drained away during the night. Instead of a pond, now there was a puddle of mud. Andrew surmised that when poking the bottom with his pole he made an opening that let the water drain off to a lower level. This let them build a plank walkway with sufficient headroom to walk beneath the Natural Bridge, and ascend the stairs on the other side without stooping or damaging the formations that hung from the arch.

A few days after the *Herald* article appeared, Major Brand returned to do another story on the cave. He brought with him a locomotive headlight borrowed from Col. E. T. Smith of the Chesapeake and Ohio Railroad. It took two stalwart men to carry this bulky apparatus on the first official tour of the cave. The thirty people who accompanied him were able to see the extremities of the Chasm and the Giant's Hall. Major Brand also viewed the skeleton and he reported that:

It was a ghastly and revolting looking object, which I consider the least interesting of the numerous wonders to be found in the caverns and will only be visited by those actuated by a morbid curiosity.

Of course this revulsion did not seem to apply to him for he admitted that he took a portion of the thighbone as a memento of the trip. The skeleton, when discovered, was partly submerged in clay and mud. The top portion of the mud was crusted with calcite, showing the antiquity of the remains. This fragile and rather pitiful burial was very easily disturbed. Even by the time of Major Brand's visit it had been partly destroyed.

Stebbins, as the businessman of the trio, could see the advantage of the publicity that Major Brand was able to give the cave. He set out to cultivate a friendship with him which proved to be a fortunate relationship for both of them. Major Brand immediately liked Benton Stebbins. He recognized the native intelligence and ebullient nature of the man, and found in him a kindred adventurous spirit. Stebbins in turn found the Major energetic and curious as well as sympathic to the problems and needs of this venture. After several hours of discussion, Major Brand suggested that he invite a friend of his, Alexander Y. Lee, a civil engineer, architect, and artist to prepare a map that would give some idea of the cave's extent, and provide additional visual evidence of the discovery. This suggestion delighted Stebbins, and a letter was sent to Mr. Lee in Staunton, Virginia, where he published a small paper, the *Valley Farmer*.

The Major prepared another article for the *New York Herald* and sent it by the morning stage to New Market where it would be given to Gordon Bennett the following day. He told of the great ex-

*The first Illumination of the cave, November 6, 1878, provided local visitors a view of the cave entrance room.*

tent of the caverns, the difficulty of exploration, and the importance of the discovery. The report was well received, and although Major Brand did not know it at the time, he provided the name for the cave when he titled the article:

## THE LURAY CAVERNS

Benton Stebbins had been trying to select a name for the cave that would be descriptive and attractive. He knew that the value of a name, such as Mammoth Cave, could help draw visitors and so he planned to call it:

## THE BEAUTY OF THE WORLD

This was not a popular choice, even when he amplified it to read:

## THE WONDER AND BEAUTY OF THE WORLD

It did not evoke the appeal of Luray Caverns, or the Caverns of Luray. Major Brand was right; the newspapers continued to identify the cave with the geographical location. Stebbins gave up his attempt to embellish the discovery and simply let the new name stand.

Other newspapers picked up the story, and a trickle of visitors from other states came to see the cave. On November 6, 1878, the Illumination took place. Two hundred people from all over the county and as far as Arlington, Virginia, came to see it. On the day of the Illumination, Major Brand could not resist going along, and in his description of the event told of the improvements that the owners made for the visitors.

> From early morn until two or three o'clock, wagons, carriages, and horseback riders poured into town on the way to the opening of the great caverns . . . though only partially lighted, presented an imposing subterranean spectacle. A thousand candles illuminated the antechamber making it nearly as bright as day. Hundreds of lights were placed in the left hand chambers, and the illuminations extended along through the great corridor in the Theatre and up to the Fish Market. The Theatre looked particularly magnificent. The galleries for the first time showed their great depth and height. In fact, every illuminated part seemed a third larger. The columns and draperies shown with grand effect, and the various clusters of stalactities sparkled with exceeding brilliance under the influence of the combined glare of light. The floors were covered with sawdust which made walking, for the first time, a pleasure.
>
> I met many parties from different areas of the country, who had been induced to pay the caverns a visit from reading the description in the *Herald* of October nineteenth. Many of the doubting Thomases were prevailed upon by their friends to accompany them, and some of the most obdurate were converted before they had proceeded twenty steps. One party, a farmer residing nearby, and not noted for his liberality, swore he would never go near the caverns, and said when he wanted to go underground he would go there for good. He was, after various efforts on the part of his neighbors, induced to come a few steps inside the door, free of charge. His mind soon underwent a change, and paying the usual fee, he proceeded to investigate. He had not been in long when he rushed out like a crazy man, mounted his horse, galloped home and shouted for his two sons.
>
> "John! Billy! Come on! Get your horses quick, and go with me to the caverns. I'll pay all expenses. You might die before morning and you must see the caves first."

Illumination Day had been a great success. Stebbins collected the admissions fee and after everyone had gone, he counted up the receipts in Billy's and

Andrew's presence. They were delighted to find that the admission fee of fifty cents for adults and twenty-five cents for children brought them $91.00. This incredible windfall, collected in only a few hours' time, was breathtaking. The had been working so hard and concentrating on getting the cave ready that they had not thought of the return on the investment.

"That sure is a lot of money," said Billy.

"Well, your father put up a lot of money in the lumber. We have all put in our time and labor. It looks like a wonderful beginning," said Stebbins.

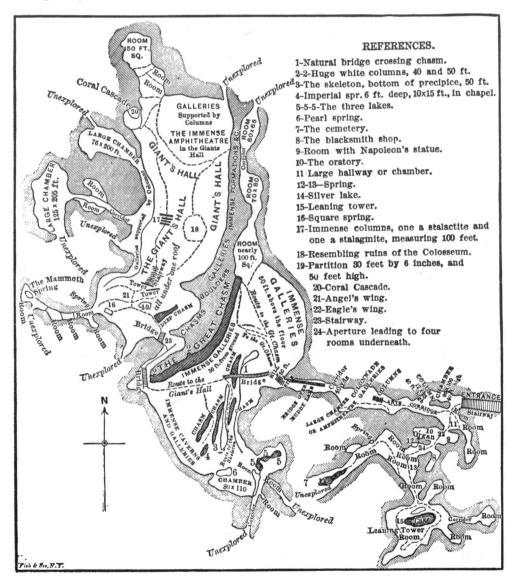

**REFERENCES.**

1-Natural bridge crossing chasm.
2-2-Huge white columns, 40 and 50 ft.
3-The skeleton, bottom of precipice, 50 ft.
4-Imperial spr. 6 ft. deep, 10x15 ft., in chapel.
5-5-5-The three lakes.
6-Pearl spring.
7-The cemetery.
8-The blacksmith shop.
9-Room with Napoleon's statue.
10-The oratory.
11-Large hallway or chamber.
12-13—Spring.
14-Silver lake.
15-Leaning tower.
16-Square spring.
17-Immense columns, one a stalactite and one a stalagmite, measuring 100 feet.
18-Resembling ruins of the Colosseum.
19-Partition 30 feet by 6 inches, and 50 feet high.
20-Coral Cascade.
21-Angel's wing.
22-Eagle's wing.
23-Stairway.
24-Aperture leading to four rooms underneath.

*Alexander Y. Lee, civil engineer and artist, prepared this first map of the cave. It is remarkably accurate; made one month after the discovery of the main part of the cave.*

"They only saw a small part of the cave too," added Andrew. "Wait till we can open up Giant's Hall."

While the three men discussed the good results of the Illumination, Alexander Lee, newly arrived from Staunton to help Major Brand, worked in Washington House on his cave map. He had been taking notes for several days, referring to his hand-held compass, and pacing off passageways. His completed plan astonished Andrew, for he had no idea that a map was being drawn, nor had he visualized the relationship of the chambers one to another.

Lee presented the map to Major Brand to be included with his report to the *Herald.* When the newspaper appeared in Luray the map became the talk of the town. Lee was, of course, pleased, but there was something that bothered him and he went to Stebbins with a suggestion.

"Mr. Stebbins, this is a remarkable discovery and the development that you are doing will make this a point of destination for thousands of people in coming years," he said, "but there has been no imagination shown in the naming of the rooms, formations, or wonders of the cave that provide word pictures of these remarkable caverns. All of the names that have been given are names familiar to everyone who has visited a large cave. We know before we enter that there will be a 'cathedral,' an 'amphitheater,' a 'pulpit,' a 'bridal chamber,' and all the rest.

"I'd suggest that you invite a committee of artists and authors to visit the cave and give the galleries, chasms, bridges, halls, and chambers names that will strike the imagination and add to the pleasure derived from their weird beauty." Stebbins agreed to give serious thought to the idea.

Work continued on the extension of the trails. Every day visitors came to be shown the portion of the cave that was available for exhibit. Billy and Andrew were unable to do all the guiding so Stebbins took over some of the trips. Soon the story of the discovery and the sights within the cave were being presented to several groups a day. All the money collected went to buy lumber, candles, tools, and the hundreds of incidentals that became necessary as the preparations for a full tour of the cave neared completion.

*Jerome J. Collins, journalist with the "New York Herald"*

Major Brand returned to Philadelphia, but his place was taken by one of the leading journalists on the *New York Herald* staff, Professor Jerome J. Collins. This man, hand picked by James Gordon Bennett, worked as a meteorologist for the newspaper. Recently he had been in Washington, D.C., preparing himself as scientific correspondent on a projected three-year journey to the North Pole. He was taking a course at the Smithsonian Institution on the use of photographic equipment to be used on the voyage. At the direct request of Bennett, he took the train to Virginia to make a scientific report on the cave before the sailing of the expedition ship "Jeannette" from San Francisco.

Collins, a huge, black-haired Irishman, came to the United States from County Cork and never lost the touch of Irish blarney. He was trained as an engineer, but worked as a meteorologist in New York. In addition, he had a love of puns that amused strangers but made some of his friends uncomfortable.

When he arrived in New Market he noticed interest in the cave to be high, but in Luray, he found it to be the sole topic of conversation. As he put it, everyone had "Cave Fever." His first report to the *Herald* stated:

From what I can learn, there is not a promising rat hole in Page County that has not been "opened up" in the hope that it might lead to the great cavernous spaces below where one might roam among the glittering stalagmites, standing like crystal monuments in the gloom, and gigantic stalactites hanging like the pendent wing of monsters from the lofty roofs of the vaults. The issue of a little stream from a rock is regarded by the "cave sharps" as a certain indication of a cave somewhere. They argue, not without some reason, that the water comes from somewhere, that it got there from somewhere else and that, consequently, the two "somewheres" in combination, acted on chemically by imagination and highly diluted geological knowledge, acidulated by envy of the luck of Campbell and Stebbins, must form a big cave on the particular explorer's farm.

In this secluded region, where people speak of going over the mountain to New Market as they might in a village in central New York, speak of going to the great metropolis itself, exaggerated ideas prevail of things going on beyond the pine-clad and sometimes, cloud-capped horizons. In the "North" as they call it, everybody is rich. There is enterprise and energy beyond the mountains which, if their influence could be brought to bear on Page Valley and Luray, would revolutionize this little world. I meet old people of unusual intelligence, who have never seen a city, big or small; who, in fact, have lived their long lives in and about Luray and suffered in the most distressing manner the ravages of the war, for this region, seventeen years ago was the battle ground where Stonewall Jackson, Sheridan, Shields, and other famous leaders fought and raided, burned and pillaged, in the struggle that ended in Appomattox.

Beyond the experiences of that cruel war, which brought them in contact with the horrible phases of civilization, the inhabitants have had very few to disabuse them of their queer notions of things going on in such distant places as Washington, Baltimore, and New York. Hence it is only natural that when something has occurred to draw the attention of the whole country to Luray, and perhaps a steady stream of visitors, the wildest hopes of prosperity in the near future are excited in the breasts of people who have touched hardpan, and think any new thing is a good thing. "Ah, Sir," said an old resident, "If we only had a railroad here what a fine thing this cave would be for Luray."

Sure enough, it would help things amazingly, but I fear the material benefits to be enjoyed would be counterbalanced by moral evils that would change a kind-hearted, hospitable, courteous, and honest community into a race of boarding house harpies.

I prepared myself, on coming here, for a first class disappointment, that is to say, I allowed at least 80% discount on the description of the wonders of the cave, feeling satisfied however, that the subterranean showrooms contained objects of much interest. On the night of my arrival, and after a hasty supper, I organized a party for the purpose of making a general exploration of portions of the cave reachable to people wearing decent clothes. I don't mean by this that a complete examination of the place requires any sacrifice of modesty, but a good coat and other garments of equal importance would be completely ruined by a tour of inspection worthy of the name. A drive of about a quarter of an hour duration brought us to the low bare hill that covers the caverns. In the utter blackness that prevailed, and the loneliness of the place, we looked like a party of resurrectionists going stealthily to despoil some cemetery. Closely wrapped up, for the night was bitterly cold, we walked up the hill to the little shed where the proprietors keep supplies of candles and reflecting holders. These were soon adjusted and each person provided with a good light. We then walked to the head of the stairway, looking downward to the cave door between two retaining walls of masonry, a descent of about fifty feet. On looking down this narrow passage, the idea of going into a great vault in a cemetery grows stronger. The place had such a weird, dismal appearence. The dim light, carried down by one of the proprietors who opened the cave door, shown with a ghastly glimmer over the narrow stairway, and its stone walls. When the door was opened, a great black void beyond looked like the mouth that was about to swallow us. Descending, however, things took a more natural shape, and without stooping, or in any way getting inconvenienced we entered a passage that descended inward to a splendid large antechamber, with a flat, but lofty ceiling, with large and picturesque stalactites of various forms and pendent from it. I use the word "pendent" ad-

visably, because in treating of this particular cave the expression has a special significance in relation to stalactites. One of these hangs over the center of the antechamber, and the point where there is a naturally formed hook, or rather barb, which the proprietors have skillfully utilized by hanging a large tin candelabra. The. stalactite thereby forms a ceiling ornament of peculiar usefulness, and I might add, beauty. Towards the sides, the walls slope down suddenly and are terminated at a height about four feet from the floor by a very remarkable formation of continuous stalactites which look like a petrified drapery folded in a most intricate fashion.

At the inner end of the antechamber is an immense columnlike mass that divides the passage. This is a mighty stalactite which has fallen from the flat ceiling and buried its point or points, (for it must have been several) in the soft floor of the cave. Its columnlike appearance is at first glance deceptive. An examination reveals its real stalactite character, even the position it once occupied, when pendent, is clearly defined above with the comparatively bare space it has left among the other roof formations. Could this great stalactite speak to us, it might tell us that it was growing old when some of the stone used in the constructing of the great Pyramids were in process of formation.

We commenced to descend from the antechamber into a great depression, whose ceiling, however, did not also descend to a corresponding level. Here we found a bewildering collection of stalactites and stalagmites of hues varying from white to brownish drab or ochre tint. Among the curiosities of this curious collection is a fringe of continuous stalactitic formation arranged along the left wall and pendent from a narrow shelf, eight or ten feet above the floor. At first glance, and even a nearer one at that, shows a lot of fish, fresh

*The Fish Market*

and glistening with moisture, hanging all along in a line. Closer examination explains the illusion. The varigated colors, pure white to a dull bluish slate color, the elongated rounded objects, the peculiar arrangement of them in relation to each other, gives the whole formation such a likeness to a string of freshly caught fish that I could not help but telling the proprietor that it was the finest "Bass relief" I ever saw. I regret to say that my complimentary remark was quite lost on him.

Professor Collins made only a cursory examination of the cave that night, but came to the conclusion that there must have been a great cataclysmic shock that caused the formations to fall or be moved from their natural position. He was informed by Mrs. Young, the wife of the Washington House proprietor,

that there had been an earthquake in Page County twenty-one years before and that a farmer passing Cave Hill felt and heard a great rumbling underground. Collins did not accept this as an explanation of the many fallen stalactites, but still attributed it to some earth movement, perhaps at the time of the "grandfather of Columbus."

The next day Collins returned to the cave and for seven hours was guided by Andrew Campbell into the remote areas that had not been previously explored. Collins had changed to an old suit of clothes and wore overalls over them. He had a worsted cap on his head and became "intimately acquainted" with the ever-present mud that covered the floor. He described for his readers the difficulties, including,

. . . The crevices we crawled through, sometimes head foremost, sometimes advancing by the rear, often rolling over two or three times, in order to make the correct turns to suit the sinuousities of the course. Really, people never can tell what gymnastic performances they are capable of, until they are put to the test. For my part I have looked back with astonishment at the apertures that I have squeezed myself through in the cave, in the pursuit of knowledge. My companion, a much slighter individual than myself, got along a little better. Besides, he had been there before and was not embarrassed as I was, by carrying instruments, for I had provided myself with a thermometer and aneroid barometer for making of some observations of temperature and pressure.

Professor Collins found it difficult to describe details of the cave. He read the previous descriptions by Major Brand, had seen the map of Alexander Lee, but was not prepared for the complexities of the formations. He made the following comparison:

The chief feature of most of the chambers is the stalactite formations on the roof and sloping walls. Take an area 100 feet square of thick grass, of which it is desirable to describe the form, length and peculiar curving and twisting of each particular blade, and then estimate the work to be done in giving a detailed description of that grass patch. So with this enormous crop of stalactites in the Luray Cave. They bear a general resemblance to one another, yet no two of them are alike in detail. The most commonplace ones will bear, in microscopic inspection, because of the roughness that appears on it, like a patch, is in reality formed of the most exquisite arrangement of minute crystalizations so delicate as to confound the observer with wonder.

Ten hours in the cave had converted Professor Collins from a cynical critic to

a believer in the accuracy of the remarkable discoveries within Luray Cave. He was therefore incensed when the *Baltimorean* published an article that

*Curious formation looking like a wrecked ship*

the whole reported discovery was a hoax; that the Luray discovery on Cave Hill was really the old cave known as "Ruffner's Cave." He sent a telegram to the *Herald* to print a statement that "The old residents here fully endorse the description of the *Herald* and are indignant at the *Baltimorean's* attempt to mislead the public.''

The *Page-Courier* also took up the cudgel of indignation in their editorial about the *Baltimorean* ''Mare's Nest,'' protesting that the editors of that paper were uninformed and mistaken about the wonderful discoveries in the new cave. The controversy simmered for a few weeks, serving to stimulate talk and interest in the new cave and also prompting Andrew Broaddus to interview Andrew Campbell and Benton Stebbins. Their account in the *Page-Courier* put to rest the various speculations.

The interest in finding another cave caused Andrew Broaddus and B. J. Grayson to hire a laborer to search surrounding lands to see if there might be another entrance. The only discovery of note was on the land of Mrs. Caroline Flinn where a pit, forty feet deep with the skeleton of a horse at the bottom, was discovered. There were no passages and no spectacular rooms. The Luray Caverns discovery stood alone as the find of the century.

Jerome Collins contined exploring the cave in the company of Andrew Campbell. Mapping was a difficult task as he found that the tin reflectors caused faulty readings of the compass. In spite of this problem he continued:

> Too much credit cannot be given to Andrew Campbell and his assistants, for venturing into these gloomy recesses. I have seen that man penetrate openings in the rock that a rabbit would seemingly have a hard squeeze to get through, and descend into unknown depths where a hand or foot slip would undoubtedly be followed by fatal consequences. He and I have searched for openings leading laterally from the bottom of deep chasms, and into every one found, Campbell boldly crawled or climbed in search of new chambers. Disappointment frequently resulted, but he has been, even when exploring with only myself for a companion, rewarded by finds of great beauty and considerable extent.

A friendship and mutual respect grew between these two men of different backgrounds and cultures—Collins with a European and scientific education, and Campbell with a colloquial, native education, never having been away from Luray for more than a few months in his life. They found a common bond in the exploration of this underground obstacle course and their daily excursions were an adventure. Collins described the difficulties they faced:

> We start to the end of the cave reachable by visitors and guides. There leaving our extra supplies of candles and such things as may prove cumbersome to carry through narrow places, we make a brief survey of our surroundings at the starting point. By the way, our costumes are worth describing. Campbell wears over his working clothes, a pair of tough blue jean trousers wrapped tightly around his waist. Over his body he draws a rough check shirt, stained with many a mud patch, but it has resisted the stalactites bravely and is not badly torn. A close fitting cap is drawn down to his ears, these useful organs being left uncovered because they must be ever ready to catch the sounds peculiar to our work. If a hole in the floor is found, a piece of rock is first dropped into it, and as often happens, can be heard rolling down a declivity below or falling directly with a resounding splash into the water. To judge the depth of the hole, we must lie with our ears close to it, and hear every sound that it made, by the falling or rolling rocks. Therefore Campbell keeps his ears open and can hear the falling drops of water, from hidden stalactities in places where no one but an expert would dream they were forming. My own costume is scarcely more sightly than Campbell's. A short and old blue

coat, which by the way, is now in tatters, buttoned tightly. A pair of blue jean overalls that can not be called blue now, for they are a uniform mud color, and a worsted cap, with a thick crown, to save my head from the spear-like pendants that stud the roof. In my pockets I carry notebook and pencil, a thermometer and sometimes a small supply of biscuits and meat to make a lunch in the most convenient hole that we can find when we get hungry. There is plenty of water, clear as crystal, to be had. And this serves as the only beverage, for Luray is so fearfully temperate in their principles that Murphy himself would have to go through a probationary course of bull-neck beef and bad coffee before he would qualify as a decanter to such a community.

"Well sir, Campbell said, "Shall we try out that new lead behind the 'organ' today? I am sure we can find an opening somewhere in it.''

"All right; but take care we have enough candles, and don't forget the ball of twine.''

"Oh, I've had a guide line a good part of the way, and we can't go astray. Take care and don't walk into that pond. It is five feet deep, but it looks as if it is only six inches.''

The latter portion is addressed to me and the cause is a round pond about ten feet in diameter, with margins of snowy deposits and beautiful folds, and a bottom of crystals. I can see the bottom as clearly as if it was only one inch, instead of five feet of water in it. Indeed, the shadows cast by the little projections of crystal at the bottom, are so sharply defined that I must hold my light, in a certain way, in order to see the surface of the water. Stepping cautiously around the margins and up a smooth white slope, along which the water trickles into the basin, I avoid a ducking similar to that received the other day by an adventurous visitor, who leaving his guide and friends for a short, but independent exploration, found himself up to his hips in this particular pond before he had made twenty paces. He crawled out a wetter and wiser man and I suppose left the beauties of the cave as quickly as possible for home and dry clothes. Creeping along among the stalactites and stalagmites, which here unite under a low roof in slender columns, we advance following the guiding string that has been wisely placed by Campbell.

"Look out! There's an ugly place. Can you make it?'' from Campbell, causes me to raise my head suddenly, to look forward.

"Ouf!''

What a horrible punch my head got from the pointed stalactite just above it! Campbell's light danced before my eyes for a moment or two, but when the stinging pain has subsided, I find myself brought up by a massive rock that almost fills the corridor. It has fallen from the roof and leaves a jagged cavity there beyond and around this piece of rock, the stalactites and stalagmites are in many cases cracked or broken off. The roof rock is crushed and splintered and immense rents extend forward as much as seventy feet showing that a powerful crushing force has been exerted here and that in places it was irresistible. The floor is hollow sounding and muddy and the little spaces on each side of obstruction, formed by the shelving down of the roof and up from the floor, are nearly filled with small formations.

Campbell has wormed his way between the wall and the big rock, and has turned to give me the benefit of his light and advice. I set my candle down as far ahead as I can reach, and then begin an effort to squeeze myself through the only practicable opening.

"Whew! What a place.''

I must rest for a moment as the exertion is really exhausting. Finally however I get through, and picking up our candles we push on. The passage does not widen, indeed, it scarcely varies in dimension, although we have traversed already two hundred and fifty feet.

"Here, Mr. Campbell, look at this opening."

"Hallow!" comes the smothered sound from Campbell, who has thrust his arms, head and shoulders into another hole and seems to be holding a conversation with the janitor of the infernal regions. Presently he comes to

and the following conversation is held through it.

"Well, what's it like?"

"I-can't-well-make-out-yet. Just wait a moment." The slowly coming stifled words accompany sounds of scraping, pounding, or the rolling of bits of dirt through the interior recesses, which shows that the hidden workman is trying to make his way in some direction or other, as it is a tough job. Presently I

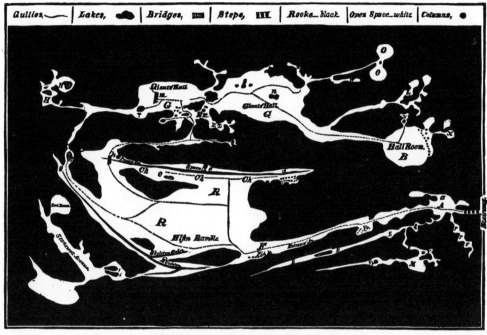

### EXPLANATION OF THE MAP.

BEGINNING AT THE STAIRWAY ON THE RIGHT.—*A*—Entrance Hall containing, at *a*, Washington's Column ; *B*—Amphitheatre, or Ball Room ; *F*—Fish Market ; *R R*—Elfin Ramble ; *Ch Ch*—Pluto's Chasm, traced with a broad black line ; *e*—The Spectre ; *o*—Mirror Lake ; *h*—Proserpine's Column ; *d*—The Balcony ; *k*—Oberon's Grotto ; *m*—The Organ ; *p*—Chapman's Lake ; *s*—Sultana Co'umn ; *n*—Double Column ; *y*—The Cascade Spring, adjacent to the Amphitheatre ; *X*—The Grotto ; *L*—Campbell's Hall ; *Z Z*—Former Bridal Chamber ; *f*—Imperial Spring ; *g*—Brand's Cascade. At *Ve*—is the Vegetable Garden. At *Em*—is the Empress Column. *E E E E*—Stebbins' Avenue ; *M*—Stebbins' Hall ; *V*—Leaning Tower ; *VV*—Bayonet Well. *P P P*—Specimen Avenue. In Stonewall Avenue. *t t*—The Twin Lakes or Brothers. *H H*—Hades ; *l*—Lake Lethe. *Z*—The Toys ; *w*—Crystal Room ; *O O*—Erebus It is not claimed that the Map is more than approximately correct as to relative distances. Very many details are omitted for the sake of simplicity ; and, to prevent crowding, but few objects are designated. The dotted lines indicate the routes open to visitors previous to 1880. Other parts are now accessible.

*Second map of Luray Caverns, possibly based on the sketches made by Jerome J. Collins and Andrew Campbell. It was published in the handbook prepared by S. Z. Ammen and is the least accurate of the early maps.*

where I am crouching and examines the hole I have found with care. In poking his head into it, and reaching his candle far in, he can be heard exclaiming:

"This looks like a big lead. I must break away some of these formations before I can get it, but I'll go."

After pounding of much hard incrustation, which yields slowly and in small bits, Campbell disappears into the hole

hear as if he is from a distance.

"Hello, Mr. Collins. It's as big as all outdoors here. Quite a fine room and some very pretty formations, can you make it?"

Then it is my turn, I shout.

"Hello! Campbell, don't roll any rocks about above there. I'm coming up if I can."

Then with much twisting and squeezing of my body I sometimes work my way after Campbell, sometimes I do not, he can go through openings easily that are impassable to me. In this way, every passage and chamber has been explored in detail. It is astonishing what a small amount of ground can be covered —that is, to say examined—within our regular working hours—mainly from ten A.M. to five P.M. The big chasm alone took us nearly five hours to explore thoroughly.

Professor Collins described his map and pledged to further define the cave beauties, but unfortunately his study of the cave was over. A cable from the *New York Herald* instructed him to join the polar ship "Jeannette" in San Francisco bound for the North Pole for his next assignment. As he said goodby to Campbell and Stebbins, there was no inkling that he had just completed his last successful exploration. The next two years were destined to bring incredible hardship, starvation, and finally an icy death to Collins on his fortieth birthday in a snowbank on the Lena delta of Russia.

Jerome J. Collins's reports to the *New York Herald* fanned the public interest and every day brought visitors to the cave. However, the weather turned cold and the stage from New Market depended upon conditions at the ford across the Shenandoah. This was not a serious blow to the exuberant owners since the work within the cave continued despite the outside conditions. Lumber was delivered to provide a wood floor for the Giant's Hall and several carpenters helped the Campbells complete the trails and stairs necessary for another Illu-

mination on December 27, 1878. Less than ninety days after they reopened Luray Cave they had a tour that covered nearly a mile of trails, providing one of the most spectacular cave experiences in the country. The partners—the three Campbells and Stebbins—were now looked upon by their neighbors with great respect and a little envy. There was no time to waste; the meager capital that the owners had was now exhausted and they were dependent upon admissions to provide the funds to complete the work.

The obvious course was to approach the Page County Bank for financing. But they were shocked to discover that this avenue was blocked when William T. Biedler filed a petition to rescind the sale of the property, claiming fraud at the time of the sale.

"He don't stand a snowball's chance in hell of making that suit stick," said the sheriff. "That area has been known to have caves in it for as long as I can remember. It's known as the 'Cave Hill Property' so what's surprising about discovering a cave there?"

The partners nodded in agreement, but the fact remained that the law suit, however implausible, prevented any lending institution from investing money. They would have to get by on the resources that they could get from the admissions, plowing back into the cave the money in the form of trails, lights, steps, and guide service. They would make what improvements they could during the winter, and in the spring try and attract as many visitors as possible. If only the railroad was completed, then the problem of attracting visitors would be over.

# VIII

The Buracker home at the intersection of Water and Main Street was known as the "Mansion." This once prosperous home and its owner had fallen on hard times. Now all of Sam Buracker's property was attached, and there was danger of foreclosure. Each of the four Buracker girls had married local men except Fanny (William T. Biedler's wife) but they were unable to stop the relentless pressure of the court to satisfy Sam Buracker's debts.

Finally William T. Biedler in Baltimore decided that he must take the initiative, so he called a meeting of the entire family early in January, 1879. The five families assembled: the Siberts, Weavers, Morrises, Amisses, and Biedlers along with the three Burackers—Caroline, Samuel, and their son, Eddie. It was a grim gathering in the parlor of the Mansion. The covers had been hastily removed from the musty overstuffed furniture to accommodate the sober group who watched William Biedler pacing nervously back and forth.

"There is no way that we can prevent the courts from foreclosing on this house—and your house too," he said, turning to face Jim Weaver. "The little house you have is part of the original parcel. There is no way we can separate it."

Jim Weaver nodded and looked at the floor.

"There is one possibility," said Jim Sibert. As the official court appointed executor of the estate, he had proved to be the most helpful of the local family. "We might be able to use the dower's rights of Mrs. Buracker and have her bid on the property when it is put up for sale. That would avoid the necessity of putting up any front money and provide the retention of the property."

"How much money was assigned to her in the settlement of the Strickler property?" asked William Biedler.

"About a thousand dollars," answered Sibert. "The court has the money and we could use that as a down payment on the Mansion and the little house that Jim is living in."

Caroline Buracker sat quietly, not entering into the discussion. She had suffered great distress since the time of the bankruptcy and sale of the properties. Her husband, Sam, was a changed man after his illness, and while he was now apparently recovered from his paralysis, he did not seem concerned about the emergency that was facing the family. In fact, the cheerful and friendly disposition that he displayed to all only deepened the concern and anxiety she felt.

"That sounds like a fine idea, James," said Sam Buracker from the end of the room. No one paid any attention to the remark. There was a definite coolness by all of the son-in-laws toward Sam Buracker. William Biedler, in particular, was irritated by the rambling and pleasant manner of the old man.

Ignoring the remark Biedler said to James Sibert, "You take care of that." To the others, he said, "The next thing to discuss is the Cave Hill property, and a fine mess you made of that." His attention shifted to Eddie Buracker.

"If you had paid that ten per cent deposit I authorized, we would never have this suit on our hands," continued Biedler. "Now we don't even have the benefit of the judgments against the property since they were cleared by the sheriff's sale. Unless we can get that sale set aside we have no way of realizing any more money from real estate." Biedler stopped pacing. "I think it is worth the chance that we can get that sale reversed, but in order for us to realize any profit from it we must have control of those judgments against the bankrupt." It was conspicuous that he did not use Sam's name. He had not been able to accept the changed man that Buracker had become, and still rankled at the position in which his indebtedness placed him.

"Jim," said Biedler looking at Weaver, "I want you to visit every one of the judgment holders and get their authorization to sell us their judgments against the bankrupt, S. A. Buracker. The terms are that they will receive one third of whatever we recover, and nothing if we do not recover. We will

accept all of the costs of pursuing the suit."

"Do you think they will accept that?" asked Jim.

"You had better impress on them that there is no chance of recovering anything if they don't sign, and we must have all of them or we cannot present a strong enough case."

"Some of these judgments go back seven years!" said Jim.

"All the more reason why they should be willing to turn them over."

Family business settled, Caroline Buracker and her daughters went into the kitchen to prepare lunch for the entire group. The mansion house had been the home for the four girls and Eddie, and had been the social center of the town when the children were growing up. The change in fortunes stopped the entertaining, and the house began to appear run-down. While it was neat and clean, the porch and exterior needed paint. The stairs and banisters which served the children as a slide and indoor gymnasium showed scars and scrapes of the active youngsters. Now they were all married and away, the house lapsed into a somnambulistic state that was only revived when the families returned to the homestead for a visit. Most of the men did not have the confidence that William Biedler showed in being able to recoup the family fortune. There did not seem to be much hope that the discovery on the property that had been in the family for years would not be just another missed opportunity of the Buracker family. Sam accepted the role of loser and managed to view the world with a childlike belief that it would all work out.

Dinner was a quiet affair. Biedler's intensity put a damper on the reunion, and it was with some relief that the brothers and sisters said goodbye to

Biedler as he caught the three o'clock stage to New Market on his way back to Baltimore.

The somber and somewhat resigned air that permeated the Buracker house was in sharp contrast to the little apartment of Benton and Amelia Stebbins. Although he was tired from the heavy schedule at the cave and studio, the sudden local recognition provided Stebbins with renewed energy. Amelia had the pleasant experience of being spoken to by the ladies of the church. She had been invited to tea, and inquiries about the gallery were followed by requests for photographs.

Stebbins had tried to photograph the remarkable features of the cave but with no success. The wet plate process was not fast enough for him to get a negative that would show anything. He tried flares and lanterns—but there still was no success. Amelia suggested that she do india ink drawings of the entrance room, although she was not enamoured of the idea. She took her easel, paper, and candles and set about to produce a sketch. Her first drawing showed the stairway and the platform that visitors would use on entering the cave. Benton then photographed it in the studio and reproduced postcards that were sold at the cave entrance. Five drawings were made. The last one of the Cathedral Room was completed while the carpenters were laying the floor.

With the first money he received from the cave, Stebbins paid Mrs. Duncan ten dollars toward Amelia's pump organ. The income from the post cards also was pledged toward the repayment of the original loan, but it would be many months before there was enough money to settle the account.

In addition to handling the money for the partnership, Stebbins had the job of advertising and answering inquiries. He accepted the advice of Alexander Lee and asked Major Brand if he could recommend any artists or writers who would aid him in the naming of the features. Major Brand suggested that Stebbins invite the officers of the Shenandoah Railroad as the proprietors' guests, and also invite the scientists of the Smithsonian Institution to study the cave. Stebbins sent off letters to these men, but waited in vain for any response.

He received a stroke of good fortune with a letter from Reverend Horace C. Hovey of Connecticut. Dr. Hovey was writing a book, *Celebrated American Caverns*. He had already explored Mammoth Cave, Howe's Cave and Wyandotte Cave in Indiana. He wrote the owners of Luray Caverns and requested permission to see the cave he had read about in the *New York Herald*. Stebbins was delighted to oblige, so Dr. Hovey took the train and then stage to Luray.

Horace Hovey, a Methodist minister, possessed a fascination for caves. As a young man he visited Mammoth Cave and wrote an article for a local paper. While establishing a place in the ministry and rearing a family he let his interest lie dormant. Now his position at a Connecticut parish permitted him time to travel and rekindled his passion for the underground. His first effort was a guidebook on Mammoth Cave. This was extremely successful and with that encouragement he collected data on other caves of the country. His prose was sparkling, his facts correct and his first-person accounts entertaining. He was a distinguished-looking man, with piercing gray eyes and a high forehead. His close-cut full beard that had turned white presented a sharp contrast to his still-dark hair. The two men immedi-

*Amelia Stebbins' sketch of the entrance stairway. Probably done before the first Illumination, as the center stalactite with the barb was used as the support for the candelabra.*

*Amelia Stebbins' view of the Washington Column in the Entrance Hall.
Probably the first picture ever made in the cave.*

ately recognized the other's love of the natural beauty of the world around him. Stebbins knew at once that Hovey would be able to help him name the formations, and his descriptions would be of inestimable help in publicizing the cave. Stebbins brought up the subject at their first meeting. Dr. Hovey immediately agreed, saying, "Christening is my business."

*Horace Carter Hovey, author and foremost authority on caves in the 1880s*

In company with Major Brand and Dr. William Miller, a local physician, a special tour was arranged for Dr. Hovey by Andrew Campbell. In addition to the usual candles and reflectors, Dr. Hovey brought fireworks and magnesium flares to light the chasm, and, dressed in overalls and stout boots, they set out.

The smooth trails, completed to Giant's Hall, permitted the visitors to concentrate on the formations and scenery. It was mutually agreed to call the entrance room column the *Washington Pillar*. To the left, where breaking and sampling of formations had taken place, the name remained *Specimen Avenue*. The first corridor explored was named *Stebbins Avenue* with everyone's concurrence. Crystal Lake became *Silver Lake*, a slight difference, and the tilted column near the end of *Stebbins*

*Avenue* became the *Leaning Tower of Pisa.*

The disappearance of *Muddy Lake* eliminated the need to provide a more appropriate name for that feature, and the *Fish Market* remained as originally suggested. The broad expanse of passage before the great Chasm was deemed to be the *Elfin Ramble*, and Hovey suggested *Valley of Death* for where the skeleton was found.

The great Chasm became *Pluto's Chasm*. A brown and white stalagmite was called *Proserpine's Pillar*. Other formations and rooms were christened with names such as *Titania's Veil*, *Saracen's Tent*, *Oberon's Grot* and *Elysium Hall*. Political expediency led to naming a passage for Stonewall Jackson, *Stonewall Avenue*. A particularly fine flowstone display was called *Brand's Cascade* after Major Brand. Other people were honored by *Campbell's Hall*, *Collins Grotto*, and *Broaddus Lake*. At the insistence of Andrew Campbell, Dr. Hovey modestly allowed a spectacular platform to be named *Hovey's Balcony*.

Dr. Hovey received a commission from *Frank Leslie's Illustrated Newspaper* to do a story on the cave. Accompanying him was Joseph Becker, an illustrator, who scrambled along after the party, selecting several sites to do charcoal sketches. These scenes, later distributed across the country, gave full-page exposure to the *Double Column*, *In Naiad's Bath*, and *The Giant's Hall* in that popular publication.

One formation needed no expert to name. A wall decoration not far from the *Saracen's Tent*, it consisted of fifty-six graduated columns arranged like the pipes of an organ.

The first time Andrew Campbell visited the cave beyond *Muddy Lake* he had tapped out a tune on it. The *Organ*

Above left: *Saracen's Tent*
Below left: *Brand's Cascade,*
*named for the first journalist*
*who wrote about the cave,*
*Major Alexander J. Brand, Jr.*
Right: *Campbell's Hall,*
*named for the first man in the*
*cave, Andrew J. Campbell.*

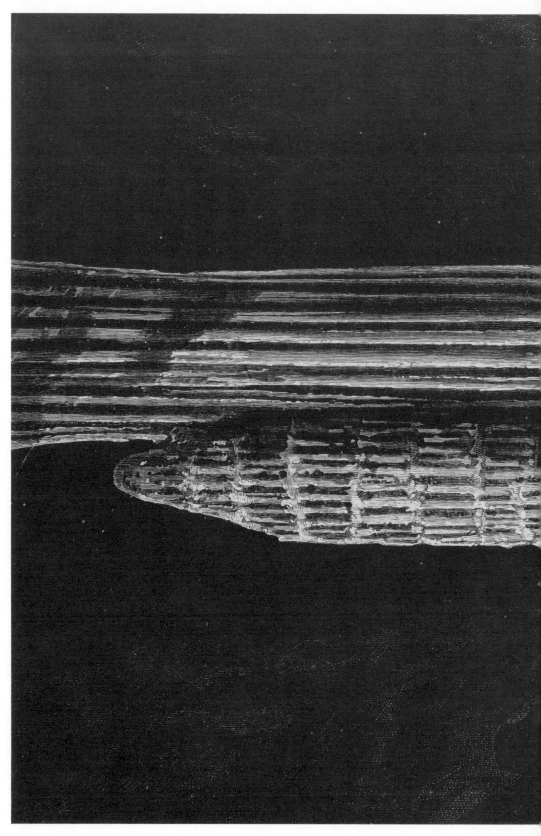

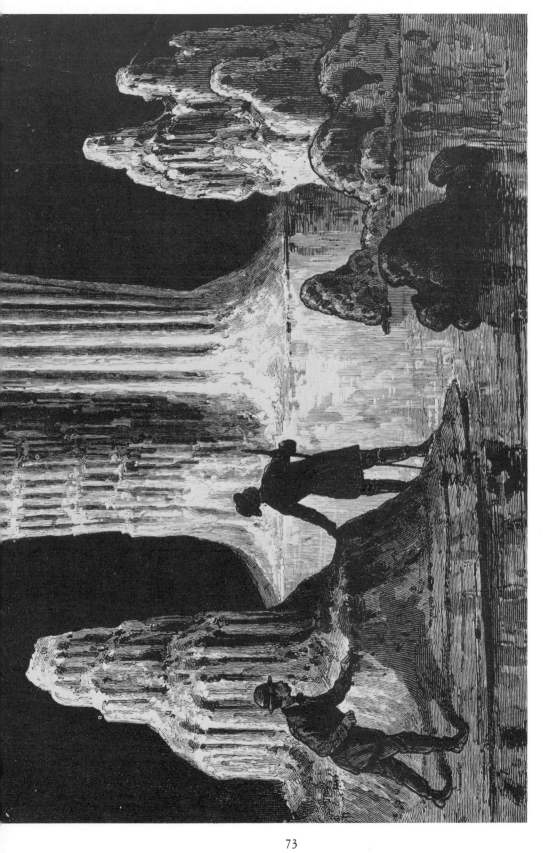

*The Double Column in Naiad's Bath, drawn by Joseph Becker. Figures might be Horace Hovey and Major Brand.*

*The Organ, the original natural instrument used on the early tours of the cave.*

*The Virgin Font*

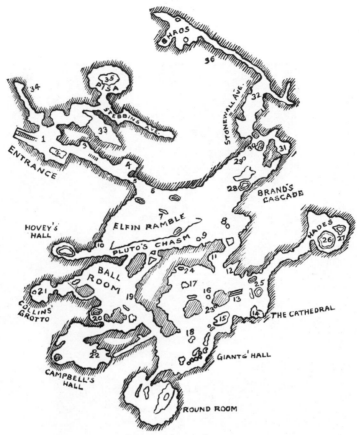

MAP OF THE CAVE.

1. Entrance Hall.—2. Washington's Column.—3. Flower Garden.—4. Theatre.—
5. Natural Bridge over Muddy Lake.—6. The Fish Market.—7. The Crystal Spring.—
8. Proserpine's Column.—9. The Spectre.—10 The Lalcony.—11. Oberon's Grotto.—
12. Titania's Veil.—13. Saracen's Tent and Fallen Column.—14. The Organ and Throne.—
15. The Tower of Babel.—16. The Empress Column.—17. Hall of Eblis.—18. Henry-Baird
(or Double) Column.—19. The Chalcedony Cascade.—20. Cascade Spring.—21. The
Dragon, in Collins' Grotto.—22. Mermaid or Scaly Column.—23. The Queen's Scarf.—
24. The Wet Blanket.—25. Chapman's Lake.—26. Lake Lee.—27. Castles on the Rhine and
Lake Lethe.—28. The Imperial Spring.—29 The Skeleton.—30. The Twin Lakes.—31. The
Engine Room.—32. Dr. Miller's Room.—33. Hawes' Room.—34. Specimen Avenue.—
35. The Leaning Tower.—36. Proposed Exit Avenue.

*Horace Hovey's map of the cave. It incorporates all of the names that he used in the cave
and was for many years the official map.*

soon became a popular part of the tour. In honor of the Major and Dr. Hovey the selections for this vist included "Yankee Doodle" and "My Maryland."

*Harper's Weekly* commissioned Alexander Lee (civil engineer and friend of Major Brand) to prepare an article using his sketches and map. As the news value of the cave was still high, the story was rushed into print. Both that article and Hovey's story in *Frank Leslie's Illustrated Newspaper* appeared the same day, January 11, 1879. This double-barrelled exposure in two major magazines helped to maintain much continued interest in the cave.

A second Illumination was set for December 27, 1878. The trail, handrails, and steps were ready for visitors. Andrew and Billy rigged wires from wall to wall across some of the larger rooms and arranged pulleys for the attachment of candelabras. Andrew made the large candle holders in the almost-abandoned tinsmith shop. Each of the fifteen chandeliers held twenty-five to thirty candles and could be hoisted to the full height of the cable by ropes.

Local excitement was high. Plans called for a dance to be held on the new floor that had been constructed in the Ball Room area of *Giant's Hall*. Admission would be a dollar per adult and fifty cents for children. There would be refreshments served, but no alcoholic beverages. Stebbins, a confirmed temperance man, insisted that there be security guards present and no one possessing or under the influence of liquor would be permitted on the premises.

A band was hired with an additional twenty-five cent charge for anyone who wished to dance. A shipment of candles arrived to replenish the dwindling local supply.

By eleven o'clock on Illumination day the roads were choked with wagons and

carriages. More than six hundred people paid admission. The new exhibit areas helped to disperse the crowd throughout the cave. By four o'clock the candles were beginning to burn out. But the

*Detail of the Joseph Becker picture of the candelabra made by Andrew Campbell and hung on the stalactite in the Entrance Hall.*

four-hour tour, including the entertainment in *Giant's Hall*, was a resounding success. Few would disagree that the cave was the most remarkable single occurrence in the town of Luray.

The bitter cold weather in January and the long chilly ride over Massanutten Ridge did not encourage visitors to come to the cave, permitting Stebbins and the group time to accomplish work

*...ne in the Ballroom, December 27, 1878. Six hundred visitors to the cave made this second Illumination a great success.*

that they were too busy to do during the fall. The mood in Luray was optimistic. Talk around the pot bellied stove in Alther's store indicated that the "Phantom Chasers" had made a smart deal. Discussion about the railroad continued. Although the rails were partly completed, work had ceased for the winter. There were forty miles of track to be laid, plus bridges and trestles that would require the greatest expense of the whole line.

for three years. With this emergency over, Biedler's plan to recover the Cave Hill property was put into action as Jim Weaver began to approach the judgment holders of S. A. Buracker to acquire the rights of their claims.

One day in February two visitors followed Andrew Campbell into the cavern. Andrew had developed into an excellent guide. His explorations with Collins and Brand had made him into a most knowledgeable man. His friendly

*On the way to the caverns*

Meanwhile, the plans discussed by William Biedler at the family meeting slowly took shape. The auction for the Mansion was held. Jim Weaver, representing Caroline Buracker, bought the property, including the little house he occupied, for $1,650. No money changed hands; the dower rights of Mrs. Buracker were used as the down payment, with the balance taken in bonds

nature, boundless enthusiasm, and learned conjectures captivated his charges. The visitors that day were particularly interested in the discovery of the cave, and an obliging Andrew filled them with descriptive detail about the discovery and first entry. He told them how they had covered the entrance with rocks and were careful to tell nobody until after the auction. What Andrew did not know was that the two men, Edgar Legg and Henry Reich, were salesmen for W. T. Biedler's Dry Goods Company in Baltimore. Their interest in the cave was not its natural beauty. Taking careful note of what Andrew told them they incorporated it in a written report to Mr. Biedler. The report gave him a glowing account of this remarkable find. It also provided him with a deposition to be used in court. Their appraisal prompted him to pledge to the court an offer of $10,000 for the property if the original sale were to be set aside. The offer was co-signed by Andrew Broaddus, editor of the *Page-*

*Courier*, and land owner of the property only twenty feet from the entrance.

The Page County Circuit Court considered the petitions filed by Biedler against the two Campbells, Benton Stebbins, and all the commissioners. After due consideration Judge Mark Bird agreed to hear the appeal. The slow process of taking depositions and answers to the petitions began to drag on through the summer as a nagging and worrisome impediment.

In addition to the law suit the spring brought an influx of visitors to the cave, helped by numerous articles in national magazines. Illuminations became weekly affairs.

Nearly everyone in town was benefitting. Washington House and Rust House were filled to capacity, since it was necessary to stay overnight before returning to New Market. The merchants and stage line businesses were greatly increased. Many store owners decorated

*The Rust House, one of the two hotels on the Main Street of Luray*

*Magnesium tape illuminating the Empress Column. A. W. McKim's drugstore sold this by the yard to visitors to the cave.*

their windows. A. W. McKim ordered a supply of magnesium ribbon for those who would like a better view of the underground wonder. T. J. Berrey, in the "Home Happenings" section of the *Page-Courier*, wrote, "Every town should have a cave; no town is complete without one."

Professor Eggleston of Columbia College in New York, with the permission of Benton Stebbins, took some stalactites from *Specimen Hall*. Mounted in plaster of paris they were exhibited in Tiffany's window in New York, leading to a major article on the cave and the exhibit in the *New York Times*. With such continuing publicity attendance increased to seven hundred visitors per week, more than the entire population of the town. Gil Zirkle added another coach to his Fast Line and advertised for a partner:

### WANTED AT ONCE

A partner with about $10,000 to associate with me in the stage line business. No other recommendation asked but the $10,000. Gil Zirkle.

Apparently the approaching rail line deterred any partners, for Gil continued to run the stage alone. With the increased traffic he raised his round trip fare from $3.00 to $3.50 and increased service to three trips a day.

"Go easy on the Fast Line!" he called to his visitors getting off the train at New Market.

Jerome Collins' prediction that the sleepy little town would change by the influx of people was coming true. Telephone wires on Main Street were thick as cobwebs on a hazy morning. The town council, taking note of the growth, wrote the town's first ordinances.

1. No swimming in the Hawksbill Creek.
2. No pigs loose on the street, 50¢ fine.
3. Unlawful to drive at a dangerous speed through town.
4. No cows at large 8 p.m. to 5 a.m.

Another ordinance admonished:

Every resident on Main Street between the houses of James O'Neil and William Miller are required to sweep to the middle of the road in front of their premises on the first and third Saturday of every month. 25¢ fine if not done.

And a final ordinance set licenses of $5 for new businesses and a charge of $20 for circuses, evidently in response to the annual one-day invasion of Old John Robinson's Great World Exposition. This traveling road show brought 500 men and horses, 80 wagons, and numerous dens and cages into town. After collecting fifty cent pieces from most of the townspeople, the circus would move on. This left a major clean-up job, and the town council hoped the new fee would cover the expenses of it.

The council consisted of five distinguished citizens: James B. Hudson, D. H. Brumback, Thomas R. Campbell, Jr., A. W. McKim, and T. J. Berrey. The mayor, Thomas R. Campbell, Jr., was elected by the council for a three-year term. The nephew of Sheriff William Campbell, he was also a deputy sheriff. As mayor he had the power to act as magistrate, and could impose fines and imprisonment for certain offenses.

With a limited number of persons providing the administration of the town there was some opportunity for a conflict of interest. However, everyone involved tried to put aside any personal interest for the betterment of Luray.

During this period of growth and changes the case of Buracker vs. Campbell and Stebbins finally came before the Circuit Judge of Page County, Mark Bird presiding. Final arguments were heard on September 24, 1879. The judge decided in favor of Campbell and Stebbins, holding that the purchase of the

*A corner of the Ballroom*

land was in conformance with the charge given to the commissioners of the sale and there was no fraud involved. The decision was greeted with favor by most of the townspeople; the Campbell boys were well known and liked. Andrew and Stebbins immediately started improvements at the house on the surface to hold needed tools and equipment. In celebration of the event a special illumination and dance was held in *Giant's Hall* which attracted more than three hundred people.

The settlement of the suit coincided with the discovery of a cave in New Market on the property of Ruben Zirkle. The success of Luray Caverns inspired and encouraged Mr. Zirkle to develop and display his discovery. The vast number of twisting and turning passages gave rise to the name of "The Endless Caverns of New Market, Virginia," but this was soon shortened to "Endless Caverns." Unfortunately the large amount of publicity that Luray Caverns received was not in turn given to Endless Caverns. It was less successful, and only a few visitors, mostly local people, went to the cave. Meanwhile the success of the Caverns of Luray was enhanced by the full-page description by Horace Hovey in *Encyclopaedia Britannica.*

*House at the entrance of the Cave*

Benton Stebbins paid off the fifty-dollar loan on the Mason and Hamlin organ, and, while he and his family continued to live in the little apartment at Mrs. Duncan's, Amelia resumed playing windy hymns with a more confident air.

IX

The Sheriff's office with its three chairs made a crowded meeting place for the four original explorers discussing future plans for Luray Caverns. They were watching Stebbins balance account books and sort through papers in his lap.

"All of the bills have been paid to date and the only outstanding debts are the three hundred dollars that you advanced for the lumber and mason work in the cave," said Stebbins. "We should be able to clear that up by April, then we will have everything free and clear."

"Well, I don't want anything from the cave after the advance is paid," said William. "Let that go to Billy for his share of the work." He paused, and added thoughtfully, "I'm not sure we have heard the last of that law suit. I heard in town that Biedler was madder than a wet hen and say that he was going to take the case all the way to the Supreme Court if necessary to get that land back. He has releases from all the S. A. Buracker judgment holders and if he can get the court in Richmond to consider his appeal we may have to go through another law suit and trial. We had better keep some money aside to pay the costs, if it gets to that."

"It's very generous of you," said Stebbins. "I think it is good that you have no monetary interest in the property while this suit still hangs over us."

The others nodded in agreement, and Stebbins continued with a list of business suggestions.

"It doesn't look as if the railroad will be finished for the summer season. We had better assume that we will get our customers over the stage routes, same as last year. I think that we should raise the price of admission from fifty cents to one dollar. We have charged a dollar for the Illumination days and it doesn't seem to affect attendance."

There was no comment, so he continued.

"We ought to have a booklet that we can sell telling of the cave's features and illustrated with some of the scenes the visitor will see. We should be able to sell a guide book for twenty-five cents and make ten cents on each copy. This will also be advertising for us when visitors show it to their friends."

"That sounds like an expensive thing to do," offered Andrew.

"It is, but I've spoken to Major Brand and he thinks he can get one published without cost to us. He knows a man in Baltimore, Professor S. Z. Ammen, who visited the cave last year and said he'd be interested in writing it. Major Brand also said he thought he knew of a publisher for the book."

They discussed some details about the trails and lighting, and after an hour the meeting broke up.

Benton Stebbins left the court house and walked to the Main Street, toward his home on the other side of town. The weather was warm, with a touch of spring in the air, and as he walked down the hill past the Washington House he noticed a sign being put up:

THE LURAY CAVE HOTEL
HEATON AND ADAMS

"Good afternoon, Mr. Stebbins," called the young man directing the work on the sign. "I'm John Adams, the new proprietor of the hotel. I haven't had the opportunity to meet you, although I've seen you about town and out at the cave."

Stebbins, after complimenting him on his work and wishing him good luck with his venture, asked about the railroad's progress.

"Well," replied Adams, "one of the engineers has been staying at the house for the past three days. He says that the ties are finished eight miles south of town, but the bridges and trestles have to be built before the rails go in. He thinks that we might see a train here in the fall, if nothing goes wrong."

"Our season at the cave will be starting in the next few weeks," said Stebbins. "That should increase attendance at the hotel."

Stebbins continued on, recalling the walk he made the first morning in Luray. Could it have been only a year ago? There were new store fronts, additional boardwalks, and a shiny new tin cup at the town pump in front of the Buracker Mansion. The bridge over the Hawksbill Creek was now a weathered

*The Smithsonian party on the porch of the Luray Cave Hotel. Photo by Benton Stebbins.*

grey, and the creek was full to the banks and muddy from the spring runoff. The once grass-covered railroad bed had been scraped and ties set at regular intervals as far as the eye could see both north and south. The tool shed had been enlarged and painted, with a new sign advertising the long-awaited *Shenandoah Valley Railroad*.

Wagons and carriages rattled over the wood bridge. People waved and called out to Stebbins in a friendly fashion. No longer was he looked upon as a curiosity because of his belief in a "Great Cave" to be found under the hill. The mild day, the pleasant walk, and the prospect that business would not only be better, but spectacular this year made Stebbins feel that his days of scratching for a living were behind. He turned up the walk to the widow Duncan's house with a contented air, and bounded up the steps to the apartment.

The prospect of continued success seemed to be well founded. The Chief Clerk of the Smithsonian Institution, Mr. William Rhees, accepted Stebbins's invitation to visit the cave. Mr. Robert Garrett, Vice President of the Baltimore and Ohio Railroad, extended passes for the party. On July 12, 1880, nine men from the Smithsonian left Washington for Luray.

When they arrived in New Market, the hour was early, so they decided to visit the newly discovered Endless Caverns about four miles south of town. Chartering a coach they went to the cave, but were denied admittance by Mr. Zirkle, who said he never heard of the Smithsonian Institution and that the cave was not ready for visitors. The next day was more pleasant according to Mr. Rhee's report to the Smithsonian:

After a night of refreshing sleep, the explorers were ready to mount Zirkle's Tally-ho early the next morning for a most romantic ride over the Massanutten Mountain to Luray. Nothing could exceed for variety of quiet rural beauty the ever-changing landscape revealed in the great Shenandoah Valley at each turn of the winding ascent. There was plenty of time, as the stage lumbered along, to alight and walk leisurely behind in order to look back over the magnificent amphitheatre. Arrived at the crest, all were ordered to mount to their seats in order to ''make time'' down the tortuous eastern slope to the place of destination. A very picturesque ford of the South Fork of the Shenandoah forms the gateway to the lovely Page Valley, having the Blue Ridge in the background.

The next morning before entering the cave with Benton Stebbins, the group heard of the discovery of the cave. Pro-

*The Empress Column*

*The Sultana column in Giant's Hall*

fessor White of the party told of the geology and topography of the valley visible from the entrance. The trip was enthusiastically received. The fact that "this was the first cave experience for most of the party" gave the report the freshness and wonder of a tourist brochure rather than a scientific excursion. Although limited in circulation to the scientific community, its contents were eagerly picked up by Stebbins and quoted as testimony to the beauty and unusual nature of Luray Caverns.

> Comparing this great natural curiosity with others of the same class, it is safe to say that there is probably no other cave in the world more completely and profusely decorated with stalactitic and stalagmitic ornamentation than that of Luray.

This bold statement from the report to the Institution provided an air of scientific approval for the cave which would have continued benefits in the years to come.

In the midst of this rising wave of good luck and good fortune there appeared again the spector of another law suit. William Biedler had petitioned the Supreme Court of Appeals in Richmond for a review of the lower court decision. Judge Joseph Christian decided to have the "appeal allowed according to the prayer of the petitioners. Bond required in the penalty of $500 with condition as the law directs."

William Biedler, with all of the judgments in his name accepted the risk of the suit and agreed to these terms. His risk would be the five hundred dollars plus legal fees to see if he could have rescinded the original sale of the land.

This turn of events was not unexpected to the defendants, but the possibility that they might lose did not seriously concern them. Everyone in town accepted the fact they were the rightful owners. Most of the townspeople were reaping financial rewards because of the cave's success. The land assessor, Mr. McCullough, put a value on the land that encompassed the cave of $25,000. This assessment meant that the tiny tract of twenty-eight and a half acres that had sold for less than $500 was now taxed at 15 percent of the value of all the land in the entire county of Page. This property comprised only 0.00014 percent of the total 193,216 acres of taxable land. Taxes were assessed at $245.67 per year, nearly one half the purchase price of the land. This disclosure and assessment created more concern to the owners of the cave than the possible risk of the Richmond law suit.

Finally the railroad was completed. In early October, 1880, the first work train steamed into town, whistle screaming and cinders flying. Almost the whole town was at the station. As fireworks exploded, bunting festooned the tracks and flags from the fourth of July were displayed. Luray was not the main objective of the railroad. The principal goal was to reach the Shenandoah Iron Mines twenty miles south of town before winter set in and halted work. The mines had been stockpiling pig iron waiting for the railroad that would be able to haul it to the mills in the north. The train hurried through Luray, carrying more rail and supplies to the men working on the last trestle at East Liberty, fifteen miles south.

A few days later a special train heading for Luray carried many important officials of the railroad company. The Hon. William Milnes, president of the Shenandoah Railroad, and vice president Col. U. L. Boyce, were along, plus many directors and engineers. Guests included presidents of the New Jersey Central Railroad, Lehigh and Susquehanna Railroad, Western Maryland Railway, and the Philadelphia and Reading Railroad. After touring the cave these gentlemen returned to the Rust House where it is reported "wine and champagne flowed freely." The fact that Luray was dry apparently did not apply to the visitors from the north. William Campbell and Benton Stebbins were invited to the luncheon, and Stebbins was seated next to President Milnes. Conversation concentrated on the caverns.

"That's a remarkable cave, Mr. Stebbins," said Mr. Milnes. "Have you considered the possibility of selling it?"

*The Rust House*

*The Honorable William Milnes, Jr., founder of the Town of Shenandoah.*

"No, I can't say we have given it much thought," replied the surprised Stebbins. "We have been so busy getting it prepared for visitors that we never considered much beyond making a succes of the business."

"This is going to be an important source of traffic income for the line," Milnes continued. "It already is a big thing for the town. You ought to give

some thought to the possibility of sale or merger for additional capital to be ready for the tourists that will come when the railroad is complete."

"What did you have in mind?" asked Stebbins cautiously.

"Well, I know there is a suit pending regarding the ownership of the land, but that will be settled soon. When it is cleared up we should talk about the future of the cave. After all, whether we do anything or not we are partners in the transportation of people, whether it is in transportation over the railroad, or through the cave. There is a good possibility that we might be able to make a plan of mutual benefit."

"We don't think the law suit will go very far," said Stebbins, "and when it is settled, we certainly would be interested in talking to you about the cave's future. I have some big ideas for improvements that would make it even more spectacular to visitors. The men from the Smithsonian Institution tell me that it is possible to get electric lights that would light the cavern as bright as day. Mr. Edison has lighted a whole city block in New York. There is also an arc light system that has been used outdoors to light up a park in Pittsburgh.''

''Let's talk about it when the line is finished to the Shenandoah Iron Works,'' concluded Mr. Milnes. Then, to the rest at the table he cried, ''Let's drink a toast to the cave!''

As the others picked up their champagne glass, Stebbins picked up his water glass, and they saluted.

''To the cave!''

Campbell and Stebbins flushed with pride and embarassment as these influential and extremely powerful men signaled their good wishes.

A noisy and exuberant group climbed aboard the special train. The Baldwin Engine #4 was put in reverse and backed down the tracks to Bentonville, fifteen miles to the north. There a turntable enabled them to proceed in a more normal fashion to Philadelphia.

Campbell and Stebbins stood on the tracks as the engine, puffing and steaming, disappeared around the bend. Exuberantly they slapped each other on the back and shouted.

''There's good times ahead!'' said Stebbins. ''It's been a long time coming, but it looks like good times at last.''

But the next day brought a delay in the completion of the rail line. An accident on the East Liberty trestle, fifteen miles south of Luray, brought tragedy.

### TRESTLE WRECKED

A serious disaster occurred on the Shenandoah Valley Railroad, at East Liberty, Page County, Virginia on Saturday last. At 2:30 P. M. the entire trestle work, 1260 feet long and 94 feet high went down with a crash in one promiscuous ruin, instantly killing Walker Johns, of Barboursville, Orange County, Virginia, and seriously injuring Stewart Bocock, of McGaheysville, Rockingham County, Virginia. Loss $10,000 or $12,000. This accident will probably delay the completion of this section of the road for several months. Johns fell a distance of 87 feet and was instantly killed. Bocock fell about forty feet and was injured in the back and hip, but strange to say, had no bone broken. About ten other men were on the trestle at the time it commenced falling, but managed to make their escape from the crashing timbers, some jumping down as far as 20 feet without injury. The cause of the accident was a heavy gale of wind blowing at the time on the unfinished work. The whole immense superstructure came down almost in an instant, and remains now one mass of ruins, a great portion of the timbers being broken and rendered useless. The contractors Messrs. Mills and Rowland have gone to work at once to repair the damage.

The collapse delayed the completion of the through train route, and winter weather did not help the production schedule. The first snowfall on November 12, 1880, signaled the beginning of one of the severest winters ever experienced in the Shenandoah Valley. By early December the ice was three to four inches thick on the ponds. Attendance at the cave decreased to a fraction of the year before. Part of the drop came from the competition from Endless Caverns near New Market where Mr. Zirkle had installed a wood floor and held weekly concerts. A ''cave war'' developed among the stage drivers to entice the casual visitor to ''their cave,'' resulting in a round trip fare to either Luray or Endless Caverns.

Benton Stebbins took advantage of the slow period to go to Philadelphia and meet with the railroad people. He had prepared a list of suggestions and brought along a copy of the cave guide book written by S. Z. Ammen. This illustrated, twenty-four page booklet had been printed by J. W. Borst of Baltimore. Major Brand had been true to his word. He must have been extremely persuasive for J. W. Borst married Judge Stewart's daughter Nettie, thereby becoming Major Brand's brother-in-law. The publication was much more elaborate than they had expected, but the extra cost was carried by advertisements that Stebbins and Brand obtained from people in Luray: Gil Zirkle, liveryman; The Rust House; The Luray Cave Hotel; and A. W. McKim's Drug Store. Stebbins proved himself to be a fine salesman for he even sold an advertisement

of smoke superimposed upon colorful rural landscapes. Mr. Milnes rose, walked around the large mahogany desk, and introduced him to Mr. Kimball, new vice president of the railroad. The cordial meeting focused on the line's progress toward Luray.

"We have engaged an architect to design a series of resort hotels to be built along the route of the new railroad," said Mr. Kimball. "It is our plan to form independent corporations for these hotels and have them operate with professional managers who will reside at the site of each hotel. This arrangement will

*The Luray Inn*

to William T. Biedler's brother-in-law, J. M. Amiss, resident dentist in Luray.

Armed with this publication, Stebbins went to the imposing brownstone building that housed the offices of the Shenandoah Valley Railroad Company. In spite of the seven-year hiatus in the completion of the railroad, the offices had a quietly opulent air. The doorman directed Stebbins up the broad banistered stairway with elegant carpeted stairs. Stebbins was impresseed as he was ushered into the office of Mr. Milnes by a spectacled, stiff-collared clerk.

The carpeted office, profusely paneled in dark wood, was tastefully decorated with paintings of trains with puffs

permit us to monitor the success of each venture."

Mr. Kimball pulled a blueprint from a rack and spread it on the table.

"All of the hotels will be built in English Tudor style," he continued. "This one is planned for Luray."

The plans showed a handsome three-story building 153 by 160 feet in dimension with turreted slate roofs and field stone lower floors. Specifications included indoor plumbing, dining halls, and other modern conveniences such as gas lighting from an independent carbide generator.

"There will be a restaurant and waiting room associated with the station," added Mr. Milnes. "Livery stables will be located at the far end of the property."

Stebbins was greatly impressed by the presentation. He put on his glasses and studied the plans carefully.

"That will be the finest hotel in Virginia," he said approvingly.

"We hope so," said Mr. Kimball with a laugh. "There will be three of them with similar design when we get through. This one in Luray will be the first, and we hope the attraction of your fine cave will provide the visitors to fill it every night in the season."

"Have you given thought to our discussion about the future of the cavern?" asked Mr. Milnes as he returned to his desk. Stebbins sat down gingerly in a leather upholstered chair and hesitated as he took off his wire rimmed glasses and put them in his pocket.

"Yes, and I've discussed it with my partners. We have had about 4,000 visitors since we opened, but with the railroad it should do three times as well. We would like to continue to run it, but with that many visitors we would require better facilities than we have at present. Some of the stairs could be of masonry, the walks paved with concrete, and the entrance house enlarged to handle crowds that will come by railroad."

The two business men remained silent as Stebbins continued.

"We figure that it would take about $10,000 to make these improvements, and when they are complete the cave would be worth the $50,000 that everyone seems to think it's worth."

Stebbins looked at each of the men. Milnes and Kimball exchanged glances.

"Do you have the money to make those improvements?" asked Milnes.

"No."

"We would have to have a clear title, of course, but I think that the corpora-tion would offer $40,000 for the cave, just as it is. We would expect you and the Campbells to continue with the association for a period of time in order to make the transition, but that could be worked out," said Milnes.

Stebbins was speechless. He had never believed that the sale of the cave would be so easy; and the serious talk of such a tremendous sum of money befuddled him.

Finally he said, "I'll have to talk to my partners, but I think they would be agreeable to such an offer."

Mr. Milnes rose and extended his hand to Stebbins, who struggled out of his chair and offered his left hand. Then he turned and shook hands with Mr. Kimball.

"We can work out the details, Mr. Stebbins," said Milnes. "We will have to wait until the decision of the Appeals Court is made, but we have a gentlemen's agreement."

Stebbins left the room in a daze. It was not until he was on the train back to Luray that the full impact of the agreement reached him. The suffering with the uncertainties of the photographic business; his gamble with the search for the cave, and the development and overcoming of the natural obstacles were nearly over. He and his partners would be rich. Forty thousand dollars even when divided three ways was more money than he ever expected to have. Amelia would never have to worry again. His son Eugene would not have the handicap of a lack of education in attaining a profitable career. As the train rocked along, he stared out the window at the scenery rushing by and mused that he would almost miss the pursuit and challenge of the goal. He brought himself up short with this kind of thinking. There was still a long way to go before the sale was consummated.

Andrew and Billy Campbell were delighted with the news. Only the sheriff offered any resistance to the offer that Stebbins presented.

"That cave must be worth a lot more money if they picked up that offer so quick," commented the sheriff. "But it's nothin' but a dream if we don't win that court case in Richmond."

Amelia was dazzled. She had never felt that the cave was really theirs, so the idea of selling it did not bring any regret. She was proud of Benton and she knew better than anyone the risk and personal cost that the cave had been to him and their limited means. It seemed unreal that their financial problems might soon be over.

The offer to purchase the cave was not to be kept a secret. Andrew and Billy promptly spread the news while the townsfolk looked with mixed emotions at the prospect. While it was brotherly to be glad for their impending good fortune, there was also a good deal of envy of their success.

Meanwhile, life went on in Luray as before. The principal local issue for the coming election was centered around the continuation of local option and the possible legal sale of liquor in the town limits. The council had enforced this ordinance, but several members felt that it would be a hinderance to the development of the town as an important railhead on the Shenandoah Valley Railroad. Under the guise of "Improvement" the political battle cry was to make legal the right to sell spirits in hotels and stores of the town.

Benton Stebbins had avoided politics in the two-and-one-half years he had lived there. His own sincere convictions of the sins of liquor had been instilled in him when he was a farm boy in New York State. Attending temperance meetings there had made him a believer,

and he continued to be a strong advocate of abstinence. The threat of repeal of the ordinance prompted Stebbins to call a "Blue Ribbon" meeting in the neighborhood, the Blue Ribbon being the badge of total abstainers. More than one hundred people responded. Most church members, Judge Stewart, and the ministers attended, and many spoke of the changes that would occur if liquor licenses were granted.

"Shall we have dens for fostering idleness, swearing, and other nameless wickedness, or be free from these shadows of Hell? . . . Shall boys find a low amusement in listening to the often indecent songs of intoxicated persons, or enjoy the undeniably purer entertainment which is found in the company of parents and sisters?"

These powerful arguments polarized the electorate blurring the lines between business and economic policies and moral issues. The ladies in the audience were particularly impressed with the message. But without the right to vote, they were limited to what influence they could exert on their menfolk.

Things were changing in what was still a sleepy town. Benton Stebbins, a relatively new resident was now accepted by the majority of the local people because of the cave's prosperity and his strong stand that "liquor was an instrument of the devil." It was in this climate of change and impending prosperity that William Campbell, the sheriff, approached his partner Stebbins.

"Mr. Stebbins," said the sheriff, "my nephew, Thomas Campbell, has been mayor for nearly three years. He has bought a farm at Mount Williams and will not be in town during the spring while getting his land ready for crop. He says that he would resign if we vould find someone to complete his term on the council. He's afraid that if he is not able to be here, the 'License and Improvement' boys will run away with the election in May and we will have a council dominated by the special interests of the railroad.''

The sheriff's unfolding idea came as a shock to Stebbins. He had become accustomed to the idea of being a stranger in town. His northern background, had, to his mind, excluded him from advancing to any important position. Now it was suggested that he be thrust into the most influential position of the community without any previous experience on the council. Despite the surprise the scheme appealed to him as he quickly realized the advantage that this would give him in the negotiations with the railroad.

''Do you think that there would be a chance?'' he asked.

''With your known stand on the local option issue, I'm sure that we can get enough votes on the council to put you in,'' replied the sheriff.

On March 10, 1881, the town council met and accepted the resignation of Thomas R. Campbell as Mayor of Luray, and elected Benton P. Stebbins to the post. This forty-dollar-a-year job included the power to enforce the ordinances of the Town Corporation and the power to sentence malefactors to jail terms if in violation thereof. Benton Pixley Stebbins, traveling photographer, cave owner, school teacher, newspaper publisher, carpenter, and medicine show salesman, was now the highest elected official in the county seat of Page County.

# X

William T. Biedler introduced himself to William Milnes, President of the Shenandoah Valley Railroad.

"My father-in-law, Samuel A. Buracker, is the owner of the Luray Caverns land. I hold all of the judgments against that property and next week the Supreme Court in Richmond will act upon the legality of its sale to Messrs. Campbell and Stebbins. My name is William T. Biedler."

The man's brusque manner and statement startled Milnes. He introduced himself to the man standing in his office and offered him a seat.

"I hold that the sheriff's sale that awarded the property to Campbell and Stebbins was based on fraud," continued Biedler. "The sale should be set aside and the property returned to the Buracker family. I have agreed to settle all of the debts of Samuel Buracker and recover that which is rightly ours."

"Of course, Mr. Biedler, but that is for the court to decide. You have the judgments with you?" asked Milnes.

"Yes." Biedler took a sheaf of papers from his briefcase and slammed them on the desk. "Here are sixteen signed statements authorizing me to speak for all of the judgment holders, and here is a copy of the order from the court allowing my appeal to the Supreme Court that this case is to be reviewed."

Mr. Milnes picked up the first paper:

I, Daniel Beaver, hold a judgment against Samuel A. Buracker in the sum of $384.97, authorized by the Circuit Court of Page County, Virginia and hereby release my claim to William T. Biedler as my agent to recover the money.

Terms: I will receive 1/3 of whatever is recovered by Mr. Biedler, nothing if he does not recover. Mr. Biedler will pay all of the costs necessary.

It was signed by Daniel Beaver.

Milnes leafed through the other sheets, all handwritten, finding them to be similar in form except for names and sums of money. The terms were all the same.

"Two thirds is a sizeable amount of money to charge for collection, isn't it, Mr. Biedler?" asked Milnes.

"I'm taking all of the risk. I have agreed to accept the cost of $500 if the case is ruled against me."

"Well, that's very interesting, but how does that affect us?"

"It's common knowledge that you made a deal with Stebbins to buy the cave when the suit is settled," said Biedler. Milnes frowned, but Biedler continued. "I'd like to know that when we win this case that you will strike a deal with me to purchase the cave."

Milnes laughed. "You are a bold one! I will admit that we are interested that the cave be open to the public and that its operation be coordinated with the marketing plans for the railroad. But that's not the only cave in the valley. Fountain Cave is available and will be on the route of the Shenandoah line. We have been looking at a proposal that would by-pass our plans for Luray and concentrate on Fountain Cave." This information was not exactly true. The route of the railroad did not include access to Fountain Cave, but Biedler's attitude irked Milnes.

Biedler sat back in his chair and in a softer tone said, "Well, we certainly ought to be able to come to some agreement, after the case is settled. The caverns of Luray are very remarkable, and unique." He went on about the cave and the opportunities it would have for the railroad.

Finally Milnes asked, "Have you visited the cave?"

"Well, no, but I have my agents who have made an inspection," replied Biedler.

Again Milnes laughed. "You certainly are a remarkable man. You come in here and give me this ultimatum of a plan based on speculation, conjecture, and possiblity. Your chances of winning this case are remote at best." His voice hardened. "We have discussed the possibility of an agreement with Stebbins, a gentleman's agreement. I doubt that you would recognize such an action. My only statement to you is that you are premature in your presentation."

The railroad executive stood up and stepped toward the door. "Good day, sir," he said curtly as he escorted Biedler out.

While this conversation was taking place, arguments in the case of Merchants Bank vs. Campbell were being heard before a panel of four judges in Richmond, 200 miles to the south, Supreme Court Judge Joseph Christian presiding. The briefs of the lower court proceedings had been studied, and now

*Judge Joseph Christian*

the attorneys for the principals were presenting final arguments. Major Newman, William Travers, and Moses Walton all presented briefs in defense of Stebbins and Campbell. The appellant, William Biedler, was represented by W. H. Payne.

When all the arguments were completed, the judges retired to chambers. The case was now out of the hands of Stebbins, Campbell, Biedler, or the lawyers. All they could do was wait as the judges prepared their written opinion. With no other business in Richmond, most of the men returned to Luray.

In an unanimous decision on April 21, 1881, the court reversed the decree of the

Circuit Court of Page County, and set aside the confirmation of the sale of the tract of land known as the "Cave Tract." The costs of the court were charged to Campbell and Stebbins.

The court further decreed and ordered,

> That the cause be remanded to the said circuit court with the instructions to said court to expose to sale again, after due and proper advertisements, the said lands known as the Cave Tract, at which said sale the "upset bid" of the petitioner Biedler, for $10,000, shall be received as first bid.

Within a few hours a telegram reached William T. Biedler in Baltimore from his lawyer, telling him of the results. Biedler and Ed Buracker immediately took the train to Luray.

Major Newman, attorney for Campbell and Stebbins, also received the verdict and promptly returned to Luray. It was a dumbstruck group that crowded into the tiny office of Major Newman on the second floor of the Jordan Building, Main Street, Luray, to discuss the unexpected verdict. Stebbins, William, Andrew, and Billy Campbell were there along with the lawyers Menefee, Travers and Walton.

Major Newman tried to explain what the opinion meant. "The court ruled that the sale of the property was not an 'arm's length' transaction and that there was a superior knowledge of the existence of the cave at the time of the sale. The fact that the Commissioners of the sale did not do everything they could to protect the rights of the judgment holders by getting the best price for the land also played a part."

"What do we do now?" asked the sheriff.

"I don't know," reluctantly answered Newman. "This is an unprecedented case. There is so much over-

lapping of responsibilities between the Commissioners, the lawyers for the defense, and the lawyers for the plaintiff that there are muddy waters to be stilled before we can tell what to do."

"That's unsatisfactory," said Stebbins. "You have been involved with this case since the purchase of the land. You must have an opinion as to how we can proceed now."

"We may not have the opportunity to act in spite of the order of the higher court to expose the property to another sale. The Commissioners for the original settlement of Buracker's debts were chosen by the court and charged with the responsibility of satisfying those debts. Their first responsibility is to these debtors. Once that debt is satisfied, the Commissioners are relieved of any further action. They are not required to put the property up for sale again if the debts are paid. There is no way we can pursue this unless Biedler is willing to put the land up for auction."

"Can't we force them to have another auction?" asked Stebbins.

"Do you have $40,000 to buy it?" responded Newman. "That's what would happen if it went to auction, and Biedler would get all of the money after the debts had been paid."

"Can we go to a higher court?" asked the sheriff.

"Yes. We can appeal to the Supreme Court in Washington, but that may take years and the cost would be prohibitive."

"What will happen now?" asked Stebbins.

"The Circuit Court will probably appoint a receiver to handle the cave until the decision of the court is acted upon," said Major Newman. "We have one possibility. That is for the Commissioners to see the property rebid for auction and request that it go for another sale.''

This glimmer of hope did not lift Stebbins' spirits. The events of the past few hours had dashed his vision of the future. The work of three years, the product of his dream, and the beautiful cavern would all be wrenched away without a thing he could do. His shoulders sagged as he felt his composure slipping away. He lurched to his feet. Without a word, he left the room and went down the narrow stairs to the street. He started walking, not caring where he went. His mind was afire with the thought of shattered dreams and plans.

Four hours later, William Campbell found him seated on a rock near the entrance to Luray Caverns. He was gazing across the valley to the deepening shadows of the Blue Ridge Mountains. The sheriff sat down beside him and waited a few minutes.

"Mr. Stebbins," he said softly. "I'm sorry to have to tell you, I just met with the Commissioners. Mr. Biedler is in town and he offers to pay all of the debts of the judgments and there will not be another sale. It looks like that will be the end of it.''

Stebbins turned and looked dully at him. Then he gazed off to the south.

"Last week I was talking to Mr. Foote in Marksville. He owns the ochre mine there and I believe that there is a great future in the sale of pigments for paint. I looked at a clay bank near there and it looks to me like it might be better than the Oxford Mine. It's for sale and with the railroad siding there it could be a great success.'' Stebbins stood up, his eyes glimmering. "There's going to be a big demand for paint and whoever gets in on the ground floor will strike it big.

"Thank you for all you have done on the cave,'' said Stebbins as he grasped Campbell's hand. "I think I'll go down and take a look at that property.''

# EPILOGUE

The narrative you have read is all true. The Beautiful Caverns of Luray were taken from the original discoverers by a set of circumstances which were upheld by the highest court in Virginia. Justice did not consider the human suffering and trauma that the verdict created. William T. Biedler provided an accounting to the court which showed the judgment holders claims to be two-thirds higher than their actual debts. Biedler retained that two-thirds as his commission, the claimants therefore receiving full measure of their original money. They did not complain about an exhorbitant commission. The Valley Land and Hotel company, formed to act as a holding company for

*View of the Luray Inn in the era of the railroad boom.*
*The Inn burned to the ground November 5, 1891,*
*and was never rebuilt.*

*The Campbell Family, October, 1906. L. to R: William F. Campbell (sheriff at the time of the discovery of the cave, here at age 72); William B. Campbell (Billy, co-discoverer of the cave, here at age 54, son of William F.); unknown, possibly Thomas R. Campbell, brother of William F. and Andrew J. Campbell); and Andrew J. Campbell (co-discoverer of the cave, here at age 70).*

the cave and hotel, paid Biedler $20,000 as a down payment for Luray Caverns, with the balance due over a three-year period. The total price paid to Biedler was $39,400.

Benton Stebbins and Sheriff Campbell received nothing for their three years of work. Andrew J. Campbell and Billy Campbell decided to stay on at the cave and act as guides to the thousands of tourists who came in the following years. The Luray Inn was built by the Hotel Company and for ten years was a destination for travelers who made the trip to Luray. On November 5, 1891, fire destroyed the building and it was never rebuilt. Hard times struck the valley, and the corporation that held the cave and hotel went into bankruptcy. The depression of 1892 was nationwide, but visitors continued to come to the caverns. It was put up for sale and remained on the market for several years before it was purchased by Col. Theodore C. Northcott and incorporated as the Luray Caverns Corporation.

Benton Stebbins and his family moved to Marksville, (now known as Stanley) several miles from Luray and bought and operated an ochre mine. It was not a success. He then emigrated to Kansas where he again practiced his profession of traveling photographer. Amelia passed away in Kansas. Benton Stebbins returned to Marksville where he attempted to develop a copper mine in the Blue Ridge Mountains. While prospecting one day, he was caught in a thunderstorm and contracted a cold which developed into pneumonia and proved fatal. He died February 3, 1906, and is buried in the Adventist Cemetery in Stanley, Virginia.

LURAY CAVERNS remains as a tribute to the courage and vision of explorers who will persevere to seek out secrets of our world. In an imperfect human world it is reassuring that the discovery of these men of vision has been preserved for the enjoyment of this and succeeding generations.

# ILLUSTRATORS

All of the illustrations were made by artists who went into the cave with sketch pad and pencil and worked in the dim light of candles and torches. It was not until electric lights were installed that photography was successful in the cave. The following information about the illustrators whose work appears in this book might be of interest:

ALEXANDER Y. LEE. Civil engineer, artist and publisher. At the time of the cave discovery he was editing and publishing a publication in Staunton, Virginia called the *Valley Farmer*. This was not very successful and it was only published for a few years. He was then employed by the Shenandoah Valley Railroad to prepare maps of the route through Virginia. His sketches in *Harper's Weekly* in January 1879 helped bring attention to Luray Caverns. His illustrations appear on pages: 2, 18, 37, 41, 53, 57, 71, 75, 85.

AMELIA STEBBINS. Wife of Benton Stebbins who was thirty-seven at the time of the discovery of the cave. She was born in Raymond, Pennsylvania in 1841. Her maiden name was also Stebbins as she was a distant cousin of Benton. She married him in 1872, when she learned the photographic business and took up landscape painting in Canisteo, New York. Her first child, Eugene Lawrence Stebbins, was born in Easton, Maryland. He died in 1880, in Stanley, Virginia. A second son, Arthur C. Stebbins, was born in 1883. Amelia died in Junction City, Kansas, April 15, 1898. Her illustrations appear on pages: 67, 68.

JOSEPH BECKER, illustrator for *Frank Leslie's Newspaper,* was born in Pottsville, Pennsylvania. He was one of many "picture men" employed by Leslie. He covered the news stories of the day, much like the photographer of today. His illustrations are on pages: 50, 51, 58, 59, 72, 73, 74, 77, 78, 79, 88, 89.

JOSEPH PENNELL. Illustrator and engraver. Perhaps the best known of the artists who worked in the cave. He was twenty years old when he received his first assignment from *Century Magazine* to cover Luray Caverns with a writer, Ernest Ingersoll. His sketches (the originals have, by his own statement, been lost) were reproduced many times in publicizing the cave. He went on to become a world-known illustrator, teacher at the Art Students League in New York, and respected artist. His drawings are found on pages: 20, 25, 40, 43 80, 81, 82, 83, 84.

GOATER. The original sketches used in this book were found in an antique shop and the identification of the artist is uncertain. One candidate, John N. Goater, was a designer, illustrator, and engraver. He worked for the *Illustrated American News* in New York in 1851 and *Vanity Fair* in the 1860s. It is possible he visited the cave in 1878 (the date of the pictures). Another Goater, Walter Goater, worked for *Frank Leslie's Newspaper* and in 1880 did a story on the springs and spas of Virginia. He might also have visited the cave in 1878. The sketches were transferred to lithograph stone and proofs drawn. These proofs were retouched by hand and the signature of the artist added in white ink. Goater's illustrations appear on pages: 38u, 38l, 39, 48u, 48l, 70u, 70l, 87.

SAMUEL ZENAS AMMEN. Editor and author of the first guide book for Luray Caverns. Born in Fincastle, Virginia, Ammen served in the guerrilla cavalry of the Confederate States of America. After the war he taught in a classical school in Baltimore, Maryland. His major was Sanskrit. During this period he wrote the *Scientific Description of Luray Caverns* and apparently supplied the illustrations. In 1881 he became a writer for the *Baltimore Sun,* a position he held for thirty years. He came from a family of military men. Two of his uncles were officers in the Union forces: one, Rear Admiral Daniel Ammen, is remembered for bringing the first goldfish to the United States in 1879. See pages: 44, 45, 62.

M. JANE BAILEY. Illustrator. Contemporary artist used the early photographs of the town of Luray to provide line drawings showing how the town might have appeared in 1878. Her drawings appear on pages: 3, 5, 64.

# ACKNOWLEDGEMENTS

Photographs of the burnt section of Luray and the Campbell family were generously supplied by Mr. O. Short of Luray, Virginia.

Most of the information regarding Benton Stebbins and the early history of the caverns was supplied by John A. Stebbins of California. His contributions of information and original photographs greatly aided in the search for details of this story.

Arthur C. Stebbins, Benton Stebbins's younger son, never saw the work started on this book. However, William R. Halliday kindly provided me with letters and recollections he had placed in writing. Mrs. Joseph L. Davies, Arthur's daughter, has been helpful with information regarding her father's work.

John Waybright, Editor of the *Page News and Courier*, provided encouragement and physical help by lending me microfilms of the *Page Courier* 1875-85. These invaluable references provided the skeleton for the story to hang upon.

Bruce Sloane, Susan Gurnee, and Robert Gurnee provided fine editorial assistance. Gordon Smith kindly provided photographs and Luray memorabilia from his excellent collection.

The management of Luray Caverns, especially Theodore Graves, Robert Harnsberger, and Kermit Cavedo, have been most helpful. Thanks also are extended to the guides and surface personnel at Luray.

Peter Kurz, in addition to his expertise at Zephyrus Press, has been of great personal aid.

Most grateful appreciation to Jeanne Gurnee, my wife, who has guided me through the labyrinth of book production.

# INDEX